THE WARDENS

THE CHAPLAIN

THE IMMEDIATE PAST MASTER

THE PAST MASTERS

CHARLES J. CARTER

Ian Allan
LEWIS MASONIC

By the same author
  The Director of Ceremonies
  The Inner Guard and Deacons
  The Lodge Secretary
  The Lodge Almoner
  The Preceptors Handbook

© 2001 Charles J. Carter

Published by
Ian Allan Lewis Masonic, Riverdene Business Park,
Molesey Road, Hersham,
Surrey KT12 4RG, England,
who are members of the
Ian Allan Group.

ISBN 085318 223X

British Library Cataloguing in Publication Data.

A Catalogue record of this book is available from the
British Library

Printed in Great Britain by Ian Allan Printing Ltd.
Riverdene Business Park, Molesey Road, Hersham,
Surrey KT12 4RG, England.

CONTENTS

About the Author

Charles James Carter was initiated into the Three Pillars Lodge No 4923 in May 1962, became Master in 1971 and Secretary the following year. In 1971 he became the Founding Secretary of the Plantagenets Lodge No 8409 in the Province of Kent and Master in 1973. He served the office of Preceptor and Director of Ceremonies for ten years.

In 1977 he was promoted to Provincial Deputy Grand Director of Ceremonies (West Kent) a rank he was to hold for ten years before being promoted to Assistant Provincial Grand Master (West Kent) in 1987.

In Grand Lodge he was appointed to the rank of Past Assistant Grand Director of Ceremonies in the Craft in 1981 and promoted to Past Senior Grand Deacon in 1988. In Supreme Grand Chapter he was appointed to the rank of Past Grand Standard Bearer in 1985 and promoted to the active rank of Assistant Grand Sojourner in 1998.

He has recently retired from the role of Chief Executive of the Quatuor Coronati Correspondence Circle, a post he has held since 1984 having been its Consultant for two years prior to that. The role encompassed the responsibility for overseeing the world wide operations of the well known Correspondence Circle of the Quatuor Coronati Lodge which is the Premier Lodge of Masonic Research in the world. Brother Carter was elected as a full member of this highly prestigious lodge in May 1992, and has served as its Treasurer for many years.

He is an Honorary member of forty lodges and sixteen chapters both in the United Kingdom and Overseas. He has lectured extensively throughout England, Wales and Northern Ireland as well as Africa and the United States of America.

THE
WARDENS

CHAPTER ONE

WHAT YOU SHOULD HAVE ALREADY LEARNED BEFORE BECOMING JUNIOR WARDEN

So its happened, the newly elected Master has asked you to accept the role of Junior Warden for the ensuing year and you have enthusiastically accepted his kind and generous offer.

The moment of pleasure and, dare we say, the expectation that we might be asked to assume one of the three senior offices in the lodge has now transformed itself into a more realistic evaluation of the office you will be carrying out during the twelve months ahead. The question must surely have entered your mind 'am I ready for this new role'? 'Am I fully confident that I can give a good account of myself plus maintaining the high standards set by previous holders of this office'?

Your response to both these questions will depend very largely on the attitude you have adopted in the years prior to accepting this new senior role within the lodge. If you have regularly attended the Lodge of Instruction or studiously studied the ritual and feel competent to tackle your new role in the lodge then you have indeed prepared yourself for the new seniority which awaits you. But what if you have not been able to attend the L.O.I. for a variety of reasons, perhaps through business, distance, or a whole host of other quite understandable circumstances and thereby equipped yourself for your new role – what then should you now do?

Before we attempt to answer this question let us go back a few steps and pose the question what should you have already learned before accepting the office of Junior Warden.

From the following listing the reader will quickly be able to judge for himself whether or not he has prepared himself adequately for the role which lies ahead. This is an honest personal assessment which only you can make.

Year 1. When a Steward you should learn the First degree.

Year 2. When still a Steward you should learn the Second degree and rehearse the First degree regularly.

Year 3. When the I.G. learn the charge after Initiation and rehearse the First and Second Degrees regularly.

Year 4. When the J.D. learn the Third degree and rehearse the First and Second degrees regularly.

Year 5. When the S.D. learn the Second Degree Tracing Board and continue to rehearse the First, Second and Third degrees regularly.

Year 6. When the J.W. learn the Installation Ceremony and continue to rehearse the three degrees.

Year 7. When the S.W. learn the Investiture of Officers and continue to rehearse the Installation Ceremony and the three degrees.

Year 8. When the W.M. learn the Inner Working. Perform the ceremonies. Install your successor and have a very happy, successful and memorable year as Master of the Lodge.

From the foregoing list you will quickly be able to ascertain where your knowledge of the ritual and its attendant vagaries lies, either you are fully equipped for the role which lies ahead or you are not. If the latter should be the case then clearly you will have to decide upon a plan of action which will ensure that you make such effort as is necessary to ensure that by the time arrives on the day of your own installation and the Master says to you in open lodge after giving the preamble to the installation ceremony "Can you, my worthy Brother, conscientiously accept the Mastership of this Lodge under these qualifications" that you can reply totally truthfully "I can Worshipful Master".

To accept any office for which you are not properly prepared is less than honest but to accept the highest office the lodge has within its power to confer and not to have learned the work necessary to carry out that office would be to perpetrate a dishonesty of the most major proportions both upon the brethren of the lodge, to say nothing of trying to fool yourself as well.

We have now arrived at the point of appraisal of our own capability. If we believe we have, through our efforts during past years studied the ritual and achieved a degree of proficiency which will ensure that we can carry out the duties of the office to which we have now been appointed, then we should indeed be very pleased that such efforts over those years have placed us in this fortunate position.

But what if this happy state of affairs should not exist and we have to admit that with just two years to go before we might possibly be elected to be the Master of the lodge we really do not have sufficient competency in the ritual which we might be called upon to perform. Take heart for all is not lost.

You, and only you, will know your own capability to learn, comprehend and retain the masonic ritual which we all require to allow us to accept office as Master of the lodge. You have at this point in time two quite clear courses of action to take and you should think seriously which would be the most satisfactory for you.

We shall go into each choice very carefully in a moment and explain how both can be achieved if the desire and dedication exists to succeed, but only you the reader know whether you have the time, ability and determination to achieve what is after all a labour of love. We must for the sake of progression state what these two choices are.

First is the decision to learn all three degrees and the installation ceremony within a two year time frame really required and whilst this may appear at first sight to be an enormous task, it is in fact not nearly as difficult as you might imagine especially if you follow the advice given a little later in this chapter. Second we can decide right now that we shall learn just the ceremonies of initiation and installation and thereby be able to participate in some of the lodge work and also to install our successor in the master's chair when that time arrives. We can of course ask Past Master's to perform the degrees of Passing and Raising should such ceremonies be required to be carried out during our year.

Let us address the first decision, to become competent in the three degrees of craft masonry, the ritual for appointing and installing the officers of the year, as well as the ceremony of installation. We have two years in which to achieve a satisfactory degree of proficiency and these twenty four months should be broken down into manageable segments of attainment. If you set yourself too high a target you are very likely to become discouraged and give up the attempt.

If however, you set yourself a manageable goal and find that it is relatively easy to achieve then your success will spur you on to a greater desire to become even more proficient. The various books of ritual contain on average about twenty to twenty four lines on each page if you take a cursory glance at your own ritual book you will find that many of the pages contain much rubric or instructions of what should be done and when it should be done, together with instructions for gavelling etc.

Such rubric invariably reduces the page down to fourteen or so lines of ritual for the student to learn. To learn two or three lines of ritual a day is not difficult, in truth and in fact it is very easy. A sentence, or a paragraph, depending upon its length should be your daily aim but not in isolation. Always start by repeating from the beginning of that particular portion of ritual that which you have learned previously and then add the new sentence to that previously learned portion. By this method you will be ensuring a regular daily rehearsal of that degree ceremony.

Occasionally, and for no known reason, you will find (and it happens to most of us) a particular sentence or paragraph which simply will not stay in your mind no matter how hard you try to retain it. Have faith, we can help you, for this is a well known phenomenon.

A very well known actor once told this author that when confronted with a part in a film or play which he had to learn and he came to the same 'indigestible' sentence or paragraph he simply wrote it down or typed it out at least five and sometimes ten times and the effect of this was that for some strange reason which we cannot explain the brain seems to retain this form of recording. If you doubt the accuracy or believability of this statement just try it, you will indeed be very surprised. In a two week period you will have learned two pages of ritual and you will be both pleased and encouraged to carry on with the progress you are making.

When should this learning take place. This is virtually unanswerable in a book such as this for it will depend entirely upon the individual. For some, getting up and finding fifteen minutes early in the morning is the best time of day. For others to rehearse their ritual as they travel to their place of work by train or car is indeed more suitable. For others the lunch hour might prove to be the most appropriate. Whilst for yet another group a quiet fifteen minute interlude in the evening, just before retiring, turns out to be the most satisfactory.

Whatever time of day you decide is the most convenient for you do try to keep that period absolutely sacrosanct so that you will come to recognise that this very short period of the day is for you to devote to your intake of masonic knowledge.

This practice, if followed, will become habit forming and you will be very surprised and dare we say delighted at the progress you will make if you undertake this self disciplined action. Just how easily you do progress in your aim to achieve proficiency in the ritual depends on your dedication.

A word of warning, never choose a time of day when you are likely to be interrupted, for regularity in timing really is important. If your work means that you are likely to have calls upon your time at irregular intervals then clearly your learning segment of the day needs to be either when you are travelling or in the morning or evening when you can be sure of privacy. For many Freemasons the regular walking of their dog has proved to be an admirable time of day to rehearse their masonic ritual. Each individual must decide for himself when and how he will achieve that fifteen minutes a day for that is truthfully all it takes to learn the three degrees of craft masonry in a two year period and that, Brother Junior Warden designate, is just what you have – just two years and no more.

Let us now move to the second decision which is to learn just the ceremonies of Initiation and Installation and obtain the services of Past Masters to carry out the Passing and Raising ceremonies if and when they should appear.

The ceremony of Initiation discounting the Charge thereafter is for most rituals contained within some twenty to twenty two pages, the Installation ceremony is contained within ten pages hence the total which has to be learned is some thirty-two pages over a two year period or if you prefer thirty-two pages in one hundred and four weeks which equates roughly to a page every three to four weeks.

It will quickly become clear to even the student with the greatest retention problem that such a target is extremely easy to achieve within a fifteen minute time frame each day providing always of course that he really is dedicated to put aside that period of time on a regular basis for his study. The chances are that in the process of learning the ceremony of Initiation he will find that he has attained a level of retention well above that which he expected to achieve and has thereby spare capacity in his time schedule in which to take on a little more during this two year period. If this should be the case the ceremony of Passing would seem to lend itself to investigation for it is after all the shortest of the three ceremonies.

CHAPTER TWO

PREPARING FOR THE JUNIOR WARDEN'S ROLE

If it should be that you have learned the three ceremonies of craft ritual by the time you are appointed to the office of Junior Warden and have demonstrated your ability in the Lodge of Instruction to the satisfaction of the Preceptor and Past Masters then it can confidently be stated that you are well prepared to assume the role to which you have now been appointed. Your continued rehearsal of these degrees as well as the perfection of the investiture of officers and the Installation itself should now be your aim for the future, but what about the year on which you are about to embark.

The role of Junior Warden would appear to the unknowing onlooker to be almost a sinecure but it is in truth far from that if carried out properly. From the moment of his investiture the Junior Warden quickly realises that he has to be ready to gavel when required as well as to participate in the calling off and calling on of the lodge, so he should ensure that his knowledge of these two important parts of the overall running of the meeting are rehearsed and fine tuned so that when he receives the opening question from the Master "What time is it". he will be able to reply with confidence "High time W.M". and so on for the remainder of that part of the ritual. So often we find that these small pieces of interconnecting ritual are not rehearsed sufficiently and can and do frequently surprise a newly appointed Junior Warden.

Brother Junior Warden should not of course leave his seat unless specifically released from that obligation by the Master. The Junior Warden has the duty and responsibility of ensuring that the lodge remains secure whilst the brethren are at refreshment albeit that it is frequently the case that the Tyler will assume that responsibility if specifically requested.

If this proves to be the case in your lodge do please also ensure that the Tyler is not forgotten in the desire to reach the tea and biscuits, and that someone is designated to take such refreshment to our brother Tyler whilst he maintains his temporary role as 'security officer' of the lodge.

The period of two years before assuming the highest office in the lodge is a very good time for reflection upon that which has to be achieved before progressing (hopefully) to higher office. It also has the added bonus that you have time to correct those things which are less than perfect as well as putting more effort into fine tuning your timing and projection as well as managing to get real feeling into the words which you are uttering. Masonic ritual is composed of many beautiful and meaningful sentences and sections, and if these are delivered in a monosyllabic tone with little feeling the meaningful content of the ritual can be lost and this is to be deprecated. We only have this one chance to impress a candidate with the beauty of the ceremonies and at the same time impress upon him just how seriously we believe his admission, progression and eventual culmination are to us, as caring members of this masonic order. It is so easy to ruin the ritual with less than well prepared responses and the effect on the candidate can be lost entirely.

You should therefore not only know the words but also ensure that the effort which you put into the timing, sincerity and projection as well as your body language communicate to the candidate the importance of his participation in the ceremony and furthermore that it is being conducted especially for him, and him alone.

For you to have arrived at this stage of your masonic progress so well prepared does indeed mean you should be be congratulated for such clear forward thinking will undoubtedly benefit you in the next three important years which lie ahead.

By this stage in your progress there may well be a pattern forming in regard to the work which the lodge has to undertake in the next two years so that you can prepare, albeit in outline form the shape of 'your year'. Assuming a five meeting year it would be ideal if all three ceremonies could be undertaken whilst you were Master and a discussion with Brother Secretary should elicit his thoughts regarding the future planning of the lodge work schedule. The year of Junior Warden is one in which you should have time to perfect those things which require to be perfected as well as concentrating on the Installation Ceremony. Don't waste this valuable time whatever you do for it is already later than you have perhaps realised. You have made good progress so far keep it up.

The only work which should be left until you have been installed as Master of the lodge is the learning of the Inner Working, this is of course restricted to Installed Masters but do not worry about this for help will be at hand in the shape of the Immediate Past Master and in his absence the remaining Past Masters of the lodge.

CHAPTER THREE

WHAT YOU SHOULD LEARN WHILST JUNIOR WARDEN

Presuming that you have planned your progress to the chair with great care and that you now have the three craft ceremonies well and truly committed to memory then you will find you now have time to 'raise your sights' to study those parts of the Masters work which are sometimes taken for granted and sadly are regarded as performable without the need to study, investigate or comprehend – how wrong can one be?

There are a number of such areas which occur in our masonic lives which we just accept and never seriously take into consideration. What are these areas?

First let us look at the subject of Committee Meetings for they occur with a regularity which in most lodges is in the order of one or two a year. To be a highly competent Chairman is not something you can learn from a book for although the requisite instruction can be given to the reader it is perhaps a task for which he can best equip himself by watching listening and learning from his predecessors if he is to show competence in the task which lies ahead. Remember that you can learn what not to do as easily as what you should do! The wise Chairman will quickly realise that amongst his committee members he will have those who are less voluble than others but this does not mean that they have nothing to say or that their contribution is not just as useful to the overall topic under discussion as that of a brother who speaks at considerable length on every subject raised.

A good Chairman ensures that all who attend a meeting have the opportunity to make such contribution as they wish, always of course without dominating the meeting.

Therefore brother Chairman should ensure that he brings into the discussion those who wish to participate as well as curtailing the over effusive brother who has at least one view and frequently more than one on every subject under discussion.

Let us now deal with the interviewing of potential candidates for the lodge. The first thing to remember is that the person attending the interview is very probably nervous for he may well have no idea what is to be asked of him or perhaps even more importantly whether he will be able to answer those questions to the satisfaction of the assembled brethren.

Perhaps if we go back a step or two we might bring a little more logic into the subject. What is the purpose of this man coming along to the committee meeting? The answer not surprisingly is 'so that the members of that committee can make an assessment of him together with his suitability for membership of the Craft' and then pass that recommendation on to the members of the lodge. What then, as the Chairman of the meeting should you seek to do upon his entry into the committee room?

The primary purpose of any interview is to conduct a meeting in which the various participants get to know the person to whom they are talking and that is a two way street, for the candidate is equally entitled (and will) form his own impression of the committee members, whilst they at the same time form their opinion of him.

The candidate should be relaxed by the Chairman with a warm welcome and an explanation of what is about to occur. It should perhaps be remembered that the candidate has probably been waiting outside the committee room for some time and will understandably have a certain 'fear of the unknown' prevailing in his mind.

His proposer and seconder have very probably been invited into the committee room to give their assessment of this potential new member together with their reasons for proposing and seconding him. He may have been left to ponder his forthcoming interview entirely alone although this should be avoided if possible.

Therefore a cheerful smile and a warm greeting are an essential prerequisite.

The Chairman could start in the following manner:

"Good evening Mr Smith do please be seated. I should perhaps explain that my name is 'John Brown' and that I am the Chairman of this interviewing committee.

The other gentlemen around this table are members of that committee and we are all charged with making a recommendation to the lodge in regard to your application for potential membership so I must tell you straight away that we shall not be able to confirm to you this evening whether or not your application for membership into the order will be successful. What we shall be able to tell you is whether or not this committee feels able to recommend your application to the full lodge.

There are some basic questions we would like to ask you which are quite simple and straight forward. I should perhaps tell you that both your proposer and seconder have given us their reasons for allowing their names to support your application. So please feel completely relaxed for you are amongst friends and this interview is by no means meant to be an ordeal for you, it is held simply because we wish to be sure that any person we bring into our happy and well run lodge will prove to be a credit to the craft in general and this lodge in particular.

This I am sure you will understand is very important to all the members for this interviewing committee has the responsibility of ensuring that we maintain the high standards which have been set and preserved over so many years. Perhaps the highest award which membership of this lodge brings to its members is that of being allowed to propose other suitable gentlemen for membership".

Now this may sound like a rather long introduction but it will allow the candidate to get comfortable in his seat and to study the faces around the table whilst listening to your preamble.

The questions which usually follow will be those which your own lodge has used to its own satisfaction over past years and it should be constantly borne in mind that it is from the candidate that we are seeking replies not from the committee members, therefore as the Chairman you should ensure the candidate is given a free and uninterrupted opportunity to respond to the questions put to him. It is usual in most lodges for the Chairman to have a number of set questions with which to open the interview after which the remaining members should then be given the freedom by the Chairman to ask those questions of the candidate that they feel are appropriate.

The Chairman should ensure that the meeting is conducted in a friendly and welcoming manner and that at no time should a question between a committee member and the candidate turn into a debate or a heated discourse on a given subject. The fact that a committee member does not like a response to a question is purely subjective and certainly that committee member should not return to the same topic unless he is unclear about the answer he has received.

The primary purpose of this interview is to ascertain the potential member's suitability for membership of the lodge and nothing else. He does not have to share our views on any given subject, he does not have to be a member of our own faith, and he certainly does not have to share our politics for such matters should never be broached at a committee meeting.

We are endeavouring to arrive at a conclusion which is basically whether the aspiring candidate will make a useful member of the order and fit into and moreover feel comfortable within our lodge and with the membership.

It will usually be found that after a few questions being asked that the candidate relaxes and a meaningful discourse ensues. Do watch the Chairman of the meeting and examine the way in which he handles the meeting for you as the Junior Warden can still learn a considerable amount from watching and listening both to the questions posed and the answers which are given. Confidence at an interview is rare but a relaxed atmosphere can be created in which such confidence can be built, the skilful Chairman can do both.

The candidate being interviewed is seeking membership of the Craft and the Chairman and his committee have a duty to ensure that the person they recommend is both suitable and will as far as they can tell make a worthwhile member of our ancient institution. This may well mean that on some occasions the person being so interviewed does not fulfil all the requirements the committee is seeking – what then? How does the Chairman handle such a situation? The following suggestion may help.

When the candidate is requested to retire from the committee room and the ensuing discussion produces a less than harmonious agreement the wise Chairman will quickly realise that he has a difficult situation on his hands for he has present a proposer and seconder who clearly both proposed and seconded the candidate in the belief that he was a suitable candidate for the order and yet the members of the committee have decided in their wisdom that he is not one whom they would feel confident in recommending to the lodge members at this time.

The lodge secretary should be requested to leave the room and advise the waiting candidate and his proposer and seconder that a decision will be communicated to them by post since further discussion is likely to take some time. This will immediately defuse what is a difficult if not potentially embarrassing situation. It may well be that the proposer or seconder will wish to accompany the candidate from the meeting.

The Secretary should be instructed to write to the proposer and seconder advising them that in the opinion of the committee, the person so put forward and interviewed would not in their view, at this time, prove suitable for membership of the lodge. The Secretary should enclose a letter for the proposer to hand to the candidate in which in a simple statement the candidate should be thanked for attending the interview and advised that the committee's decision was that his application should not at this time be recommended to the full lodge. Please note there is no duty whatsoever to give reasons and this brief letter should be strictly non controversial.

From the foregoing it can be seen that it is always wise to interview a candidate for membership before his application form has been read in open lodge for the simple reason that if he should not meet with the approval of the interviewing committee and his application form has already been read then an embarrassing situation for his proposer and seconder can result.

Acting as the Chairman of any committee and learning how to handle its business as well as its members is not something for the newly appointed Master to embark upon without training, even if that training should be simply watching, noting and remembering during the years of his service on that lodge committee.

Second let us look at the other very important and yet often neglected aspect of the work of the Master namely the Festive Board.

How often we attend an Installation meeting carried out with considerable competence, with the incoming Master installing his officers with a high degree of proficiency but who, upon arriving at the Festive Board and finding himself confronted with the official toast list, looks at it as though it is written in Chinese, having not a clue as to the correct pronunciation of the names or the content of the list itself or for that matter who does what and more importantly when ?

He has apparently not been given any instruction whatsoever on how he should propose the various toasts, which should be grouped together and which honorific titles should or should not be included.

How can a brother be allowed to arrive at the highest office in the lodge after possibly some ten to fifteen years of service and be so patently ill-equipped for the task which confronts him?

It is an excellent plan for every Master-elect to be taken through the Festive Board proceedings from start to finish commencing with the list of those with whom he wishes to take wine. Caution should be used in extending his list beyond four or five, for the object is to include everyone but not to interrupt what should be the major opportunity for the brethren to indulge in social intercourse.

The Master of a lodge has a duty to ensure that the after proceedings are conducted with dignity and due decorum. He should ensure that once he gavels, silence is immediate. The over-frequent use of the gavel is to be discouraged for such annoying interruptions have entirely the reverse effect to that for which the festive board is held, namely to allow the brethren to join together in conversation and mutual fellowship. The Master should retain the gavel in his possession and not allow anyone else to use it. He is the only one who has the authority to call the brethren to order whether it be in lodge or at the Festive Board.

Ideally the taking of wine should be undertaken between the first and main courses of a meal and if the following list is adopted we are quite sure it will meet with approval by the brethren and minimise gavelling.

In time this will become known by the members as a short interlude in the Festive Board procedure and that once these 'takings of wine' are completed there will be no further interruption to the proceedings before the 'official toasts' are commenced after the coffee has been served.

1. The Master with everyone.
2. The Master with Grand Officers
3. The Master with the Initiate (if appropriate).
4. The Master with the Visiting Brethren.
5. The Master with the Past Masters & Officers of the Lodge.
6. The Master with the Master-elect (Election night only).

The order in which these toasts are taken may vary according to local custom and practice. For example it may be the custom of the lodge to use number five on installation nights only. Turning now to the Official Toast list it is essential that any brother hoping to assume the highest office in the lodge should be taken through it several times perhaps starting whilst he occupies the office of Junior Warden. No brother should ever be allowed to arrive at his first Festive Board as the Master of the lodge untried and untrained in the use of the Toast list. Ensure that military and honorific titles are omitted, except where civil titles and honorifics are sanctioned by local custom and practice or are recommended by Grand Lodge or the Provincial or District Grand Lodge in which the lodge is situated.

The subject of 'masonic fire' if given in your lodge should be handled with great care and due decorum. The Master should be instructed that when giving masonic fire it is never speeded up to the point whereby there is competition to see who can finish first and the senior and perhaps older brethren are not only unable to participate but also become annoyed with the younger members for their apparent disrespect to the Sovereign, the Grand Master, the Craft and the Lodge.

As Junior Warden you should remember that it will be your duty when you are the Master to unite and not divide the lodge. You will have a heavy responsibility to ALL the members both young and old alike. Brother Junior Warden should remember in advance of his future promotion that he has a further duty when he is Master to ensure that the Festive Board is conducted with a clear timetable in mind. The members have a right to expect that their time is not wasted and that the proceedings will be conducted with the minimum of time-consuming activities so that those who have trains to catch or long journeys to make are not forced to leave before the proceedings are ended.

The ideal length of speeches, when given, should be no longer than three to four minutes. Longer speeches will frequently result in brethren turning to their neighbours to talk and the courtesy and dignity of the occasion is lost.

The foregoing suggested Festive Board training should be included in your overall plan for this year of work. It cannot be stated too clearly or too often that to have an excellent ceremony performed within the lodge room but followed by an uncontrolled and ill-prepared Festive Board is a great disappointment to the members and their guests. Moreover it demonstrates most glaringly that the Master has put all his effort into learning the ritual, but for the remainder of his responsibilities at the lodge meeting he has paid little attention to the necessity for undertaking proper training.

CHAPTER FOUR

WHAT YOU SHOULD HAVE ALREADY LEARNED BEFORE BECOMING SENIOR WARDEN

Any brother aspiring to become master of his lodge will naturally be expected to have a high degree of competency in masonic ritual and this applies none the less to brother Senior Warden for within a year after his investiture brother Senior Warden will have to answer the question in open lodge, "Can you my worthy brother accept the Mastership of this lodge under those qualifications", we are sure that no brother would willingly answer YES to that question if in his heart he knew he was not capable of carrying out the office with capability and diligence. What then should you have already learned by the time you reach the office of Senior Warden?

You should ideally have achieved a considerable competence in performing the three degrees of craft masonry. You should be able to conduct the festive board proceedings with decorum and dignity and have a comprehensive understanding of the official toast list. You should have a reasonable idea of the progress of the other members of the lodge some of whom will be forming your team of officers for the year of your Mastership. This in turn will mean that you will need to achieve a regular attendance at the Lodge of Instruction as well as maintaining an ongoing working relationship with the Preceptor whose advice in the area of officer selection can be invaluable.

Hopefully you will have already learned the investiture of your potential officers and also the delivery of the second degree tracing board. If the answer to these suggested levels of ability should be yes, I have learned them, then perhaps the installation of your successor as Master is the next area for your attention. No, it is not too early to learn this part of the ritual even though you yourself have yet to be elected and subsequently installed as Master.

It is frequently the case that when a Grand Lodge Certificate has to be presented to a recently raised brother that a Past Master of the lodge is asked to carry out this task. Just occasionally it is a nice action for the Master to attend to this part of the programme himself especially if the candidate to whom it is to be presented is particularly well known to him.

This is by no means mandatory but it is a useful addition to your overall masonic attributes and what is more it demonstrates that you have a determination to be seen as an active Master and not one who simply hands out all his work to other brethren. These then are but some of the most fundamental requirements which the incoming Senior Warden should have for he is in effect so close to the Master's chair as to be the Master 'in waiting'. Capable of doing the job at this time but using this final year to fine tune his ritual and attend to those areas of possible weakness which he will know require his attention.

A frequently forgotten part of the ritual is the address to the Master on the night of his Installation. Although brother Senior Warden still has to listen to the address being given to him it is nevertheless a useful acquisition to have this relatively short but important piece of ritual 'under control' before he is installed into the chair of King Solomon in twelve months time. It is also an important element of his education to understand and appreciate the meaning of the words used in this particularly descriptive piece of ritual which sets out the Master's responsibilities in a way that is not equalled anywhere else in his book of ritual.

CHAPTER FIVE

PREPARATION FOR THE SENIOR WARDEN'S ROLE

So you have accepted the invitation to become the Senior Warden of the lodge just one short step away from the most responsible office the members of the lodge have in their power to confer on you.

The thoughts which must surely be going through your mind at this time will be more connected with the year which you will be spending as Master of the lodge perhaps more than the year which lies directly ahead of you as Senior Warden. This is a perfectly understandable reaction for after all your progress through the lodge from Steward onwards has been directed at the one sole target of becoming the Master of the lodge and now you are so close and perhaps more importantly are also fully qualified having served as Junior Warden for twelve months to become the Master should the circumstances so present themselves, this is a fact frequently forgotten by those who have completed their year as Junior Warden.

How then should you use this period of twelve short months to maximum advantage?

The simple answer to this question is 'by being completely and totally honest with yourself'. A simple and short answer but one to which only you the reader can fully respond. Only you know your strengths and weaknesses, only you know your shortcomings and only you know those areas of your overall capability which require the maximum amount of work to bring them fully up to standard. Start then by making a list of those things upon which you need to improve or on which you need advice, by so doing you will be admitting you have a problem in certain areas and moreover highlighting that problem.

Such problems may not be large so don't over magnify them. Frequently an evening spent with the Preceptor or your predecessor can and will produce the help you require. It is doubted by this author if there has ever been a member of the craft who has not found some aspect of the ritual more difficult to absorb than the rest and the problem will undoubtedly be different amongst each of us. You have already taken the largest and most important step by admitting you have a problem, the solution will in comparison be relatively simple.

If you have difficulty with a particular phrase or group of words it is sometimes useful to break them down into manageable sets of five or six words which are easily remembered and concentrate on this small grouping until you have them fully committed to memory, you can then move on to the next five or six words and so on.

For some the repeated writing of such groups or phrases works better. There are brethren of this author's acquaintance who were able to visualise a page of ritual and virtually read it from the page as retained in their memory. Time and patience will always overcome such shortcomings.

To admit a deficiency and to take such remedial action as is necessary to overcome that problem is a clear indicator of a member who cares about his work and perhaps most of all will instill in his members when he is the Master the same type of dedication he himself has shown towards his office and his lodge.

If you are given an invitation to propose a toast at the festive board accept the opportunity to do so for it will improve your confidence, your speaking ability and most of all afford your fellow brethren the chance to appreciate how much you have grown in masonic stature and confidence during your years leading up to the chair.

Your demeanour during this period of your masonic progression should be less frivolous than perhaps has been the case, for in twelve short months the lodge members will be called upon to make a judgement regarding your suitability to lead the lodge throughout the next year and for that role they will expect dignity competence and devotion – you are under the spotlight so watch your every move. A wise Senior Warden will prepare a small set of speeches so that if asked at short notice he is fully prepared for the task ahead. The moral here is to think ahead and prepare for what might and probably will occur.

CHAPTER SIX

WHAT YOU SHOULD LEARN WHILST SENIOR WARDEN

You now sit facing the Worshipful Master ready to acknowledge his gavel the moment he sounds to order in the East. Your brain is full of masonic ritual you are fine tuned to your responsibilities, you are an experienced committee member and have a knowledge of how such committees operate and moreover how they should be chaired. What then can possibly be left for you to learn?

This is an excellent time to change books – your ritual book can be put to one side whilst you take the time to acquaint yourself with the rules contained within the Book of Constitutions for you have after all been in possession of a copy since the day of your initiation have you not?

The question you must address at this time is 'have I kept my Book of Constitutions up to date with all the amendments which have been issued since I was first Initiated'?

It is doubted if there is one Senior Warden in a hundred who can answer yes to that question – the answer therefore is to obtain a totally new book (they are not expensive) and insert all the amendments that you receive with it, you can then commence your year sure in the knowledge that you have a Book of Constitutions on which you can rely completely and not an out-of-date ten year old copy whose equally out of date rules will surely give you the wrong information.

Preparing for your year as Master is the first sign of dedication. Do not rely on Brother Secretary for it is you and no one else who has to rule and guide the lodge during the year of your Mastership.

To return to the Book of Constitutions it is not suggested for one moment that you learn anything by heart but rather that you should know precisely under which heading to look should a problem arise during your year in office.

All too often a Master will arrive at the occasion of his installation well skilled in the ritual but lacking virtually any knowledge of the Book of Constitutions,wrongly believing that should any reference to it be needed then Brother Secretary will of course provide the necessary input to the discussion in hand.

The Master should always remember that he has answered yes to the question 'can you conscientiously undertake the management of this lodge under those qualifications', clearly if he has little or no knowledge of the Book of Constitutions which is in effect the rule book by which the lodge operates then he has in fact been guilty of misleading the lodge as to his capability.

Let us then look at some of the rules which should be studied and which will most probably become the subject of use during your year in the Master's chair.

Officers. An officer who dies during the year should be replaced at the earliest opportunity and this can be done at the next regular meeting of the lodge by the D.C., asking the Master whom he appoints to the office of ... just as he would at an installation meeting. If it should be the Tyler who for whatever reason can no longer continue the Master can simply 'appoint' one of the members to the office (thus complying with the requirements of rules 104 and 113) irrespective of the fact that a 'stand-in' Tyler has been secured for the actual purpose of Tyling the lodge. The stand-in if deemed suitable can then be elected in the usual manner at the next regular election as stated in the by-laws of the lodge. What must not happen is for the lodge to operate without a designated and appointed Tyler – see rule 113. For details of a similar situation affecting the Treasurer see rule 112.

Lodge Property. The Master and Wardens are responsible for the property owned by the lodge although we are sure that many Masters will be quite unaware of this responsibility for the entire period of holding both the office of Warden and Master. You should acquaint yourself with rule 143.

Lodge Warrant. Examination of rule 101 will show that the Lodge Warrant must be present and also be produced at every meeting of the lodge. The word produced has a variety of interpretations.

In older lodges where the Warrant can be over two hundred years old it is recommended that it is not opened at every meeting but rather retained in its container. The Warrant is of course the property of the Grand Master and not, as is so frequently believed, the property of the lodge. The Master holds it in trust for the Grand Master during the period of his Mastership and then passes it to his successor thus relieving himself of the responsibility. It is a wise Master who makes quite sure that his successor appreciates the responsibility he now assumes.

The Master therefore has the responsibility of ensuring that the Warrant is present he does not necessarily have to remove it from its case and display it to the brethren as is so frequently seen to occur. It should be remembered that a Centenary Warrant only gives authority for the wearing of the centenary jewel and is not a substitute for the original warrant which is the authority the Master has for holding the meetings and initiating, passing and raising of masons.

Exclusion of a Member. Rule 181 should be read and understood fully for it will frequently be the case that the lodge has a by-law by which it excludes a brother for non-payment of subscription for a period which is less than the Grand Lodge mandatory period of two years as laid down in rule 148. There may be other reasons for the lodge wishing to exclude a brother and this rule states quite clearly how the process of achieving this desired state should be carried out.

In order that no future recrimination can be made this rule should be applied most precisely. The foregoing are but a few examples of the important rules covering the management of the lodge for which the Master is responsible and no Master should ever fall into the trap of believing that it is the Secretary who is responsible for the due observance of the Book of Constitutions. Read, learn (not memorize) and inwardly digest the Book of Constitutions it can and will assist you in your 'ruling and governance of the lodge' and you will thereby demonstrate to the brethren, who have elected you, that you have taken your role seriously and are suitably equipped to undertake any difficulty which might arise during your period of Mastership.

Remember that the Secretary might well have a greater knowledge of the Book of Constitutions due to his period of service in that office but it is quite wrong for any Master to rely on the Secretary to provide answers to any and every subject which requires reference to that book to be made during his year in office. By all means seek confirmation of your understanding of any situation but you should have a firm knowledge of the rules by which our order is governed if you are to be seen as a competent and forward thinking leader of your lodge.

CHAPTER SEVEN

ASSISTING THE MASTER

Having been appointed and invested as the Senior Warden you are now almost within sight of the day of your own election as the next Master and therefore you should endeavour to work even more closely with the current Master of the lodge. The wise Master will discuss in detail with you the agenda for each meeting and you in your turn should remember to extend a similar courtesy to your Senior Warden when you eventually occupy the Master's chair.

Since you are seated directly in line of sight with the Master your attention to his every request should be automatic and you will, by keeping your gaze in his direction, be able to follow his gavel instructions without any noticeable gap in the proceedings.

Everythlng you have done so far in the lodge has been a form of preparation for the highest office which can be conferred on you by the membership.

Don't be afraid to enquire of the Master if there is anything you can do to assist him in any way and do this at every meeting or better still before each meeting, the thought will be appreciated, of this I can assure you. Being the Master is a lonely role and the thought that there is someone out there willing to help you in any way he can will do much to make the Master gain confidence and feel he is well supported – it does help, especially when you are new in the role, that is a promise.

Time is by now very short, for you will within a meeting or so find the brethren voting for the 'new' Master and yes this is you. The life in the year of a lodge is much shorter than the average member realises. Once the summer months have been eliminated there are usually only two or three working meetings in the year which a Master serves.

Remove from that the installation meeting and the election meeting and you will quickly realise that twelve months it might be in terms of time, but as the Master you tend to live your year one meeting ahead and, such is the nature of events, that before you realise it you are planning to install your successor as Master of the lodge. Any Past Master you care to speak to will tell you that his year was the shortest twelve months of his life, and so will yours be – believe me! The second thing he will tell you is that given the chance he could have given a better account of himself – such is the nature of human beings.

Remember this, for you will surely find yourself saying very much the same when your year comes to an end.

CHAPTER EIGHT

SO YOU
HAVE BEEN
ELECTED AS MASTER

Congratulations Master Elect, the big day has finally arrived and you can now 'officially' ask those brethren whom you wish to appoint to office during your year if they are willing to accept office (we assume of course that they are able to perform the office you are offering to them, for otherwise you would not be approaching them would you)?

Yes, your year starts right here in making your first decisions, decisions, no doubt you have spent time and effort in planning throughout the twelve months just completed. When one selects officers one has to do so with the greatest care and the prime reason in so appointing anyone should be their competency in carrying out the office you have offered to them, not because they are a close friend, relative or work colleague. You have a duty now to do the right thing for the lodge, over which you are going to preside during the next twelve months. Think your decisions through very carefully for you will be judged on your first actions and this is before you are installed as Master. Take advice by all means but make up your own mind, for very shortly you will be in charge and what is more responsible for the lodge, its officers, its ceremonies and its membership, a heavy responsibility for anyone – and very shortly it will be all yours! Just a final thought – the night of your installation will be an occasion filled with emotion, excitement and exhilaration and so it should be. Remember that if it had not been for your proposer and seconder you would not now be in the chair of the Master. Ensure when you prepare your response to the toast to you at the festive board that you mention both of the aforementioned brethren and any others who have played an instrumental part in your progress and final arrival at the Master's chair. Remember that it is courteous to say thank you even if its for an action taken ten or more years before.

There is only one thing left to say to you – have a very happy year in office and make every minute of your year as memorable as possible, for its a year you will have to live with and have happy memories of for the rest of your life.

THE
CHAPLAIN

CHAPTER ONE

PREPARATION FOR OFFICE

Reading from the official list of officers in the Book of Constitution it will immediately be seen that the brother who holds this permissive office in his lodge occupies an exceedingly honourable and indeed senior position, ranking first in order after the three principal officers. He takes precedence over both the Secretary and the Treasurer, neither the Minute Book or the Cash Book being allowed to hold a higher place in Masonic estimation than the Volume of the Sacred Law. To further emphasize the importance of his office, his jewel or emblem is the first great light in Freemasonry, mounted on a triangle, the symbol of perfection. Light in its turn supported by the Shekinah or the Glory of the Lord. The writer is well aware that this is not the description furnished by the Book of Constitutions, which is somewhat meagre. Officially the Chaplain's jewel is a 'book' on a triangle, surrounded by a glory. But the former explanation is more in keeping with Masonic teaching.

There have been Grand Chaplains, (for many years there were two) since the 1st May 1775, which was the date when the foundation-stone of the first Freemasons' Hall in London was laid. Since that time the list of Grand Chaplains has included very distinguished names indeed from the highest posts in the Anglican Church. The Grand Chaplain shares with certain other high ranking Grand Officers the distinction of being described as 'Very' Worshipful.

The Constitutions of the United Grand Lodge of England prescribe that Grand Chaplains 'shall attend the quarterly communications and other meetings of Grand Lodge, and there offer up solemn prayer, suitable to the occasion, as established by the usage of the Fraternity'.

The form of prayer used at the opening and closing of Grand Lodge is apparently left to the discretion of the brother who officiates, a liberty which is NOT extended to the Chaplain of a private lodge, where the exact words of the prayer are as much a part of the ritual as are those of the Obligation. Besides the obvious duty of offering prayer, the Grand Chaplain may be called upon to take a very active part in the Consecration of new Lodges, especially within the London area where there are no Provincial Officers. Such of his duties as fall under this heading differ in no way from similar duties for which the Provincial Grand Chaplain is responsible, and they will therefore be described in a subsequent chapter, when that officer's functions come to be grouped and described.

Today few lodges have the benefit of the services of an ordained clergyman and in the world in which we live it would not appear that this situation is likely to change substantially in the foreseeable future. Masters of lodges are therefore faced with the choice of two alternatives namely appointing a suitable member to fill the office or leaving the office unfilled with the Master delivering the usual prayers during the various parts of the ceremonies. Assuming that which is most usual applies to your lodge and the Master has asked you to undertake this highly important office, and moreover that you have accepted with gratitude, you quite understandably have certain reservations about your ability to perform this important and highly visible role especially when times of adversity visit themselves upon your lodge.

That it requires of the brother being so appointed a dedication and devotion to the role cannot be in doubt for this is one office which exacts of its incumbent many years of service in the lodge as well as an acquired wide knowledge of Freemasonry generally.

What then should the newly made Chaplain seek to achieve having accepted both the office and the responsibility which accompanies this high position.

Most if not all newly appointed Chaplains have an indication well before the installation meeting that they are to be so appointed and usually have ample time in which to prepare for their period of office. How then should the newly appointed Chaplain start to put together his portfolio of accoutrements so that he can meet the challenges which lie ahead of him.

Clearly it will benefit him in no small measure if he lists the the various occasions on which his participation is required and thereby provides a small but comprehensive selection of appropriate words to cover each occasion. We already know of course that degree ceremonies will require his involvement as will his participation at the Festive Board after the meetings are concluded. A suitable selection of graces before dining commences can be collected and collated and to have a different grace at each meeting is both exhilarating and gives your lodge an air of differential ambience.

The Chaplain who thinks about his work and provides the necessary fundamental tools with which to carry it out is a valued and indeed prized member and the lodge will be duly grateful to have such a capable and thoughtful officer carrying out this important office.

For a lodge to have a dedicated and devoted Chaplain says much for its overall management, indeed it is respectfully suggested that such an appointment should only ever be made after considerable thought and discussion with the more senior past masters of the lodge.

CHAPTER TWO

THE DIGNITY
OF THE OFFICE

The brother who is appointed to this office should be one who is fully sensible to the gravity and responsibility of the office, he may be expected to possess a somewhat staid demeanour. Such a brother should be one to whom the younger brethren would not unnaturally turn to for example and advice and furthermore he should ideally be a brother of good education who has already, during his service within the lodge, proved beyond all doubt his suitability for the new role to which he has been appointed.

It is preferable, if possible, for the brother so appointed to have a wealth of masonic experience as well as masonic knowledge for such a brother will unquestionably be looked up to by the junior brethren of the lodge.

The office of Chaplain does not fall within the line of promotion usually associated with progress in a lodge and it is frequently the case that the brother appointed to this office holds it for many years and becomes in the process thereof a valuable elder statesman of his lodge. It is usual in most lodges under the United Grand Lodge of England for the brother so appointed to the office of Chaplain to already be a Past Master of some years standing whose knowledge and experience are called upon when the office falls vacant for whatever reason Very occasionally a lodge is fortunate to have the services of an ordained clergyman and such a brother can of course be appointed without the requirement for him to have served the office of Master. Indeed it should be made quite clear at this juncture that the honour of having been Master of a lodge is most definitely not a prerequisite to appointment as Chaplain and it is often the case that a licensed lay-reader will fill this office with credit and ability but such occasions are however rare but should be maximised to the benefit of the lodge whenever and wherever they arise.

A brother who holds the office of Chaplain is and indeed should be regarded as a wise member of the craft, for the office does in itself frequently call for personal assistance to a lodge member who may have a family or personal problem which is causing him distress and worry.

The Chaplain should be of sufficient experience and demeanour for a brother so concerned or worried to be able to approach and seek advice, assistance or generally be pointed in the right direction where the problem may be assisted and the situation crystalised and clarified so that the member concerned is once again free of worry or at the very least knows that his problem is in the process of being resolved with the help of the Chaplain of his lodge.

To accept the office of Chaplain the brother so approached should realise that his duties extend far beyond the simple reciting of the prayers in the lodge and that his overall stature as the lodge Chaplain will place him in a sphere removed from the general cut and thrust of lodge affairs. He will henceforth be thought of as a voice of experience both in the craft and in life generally and as a friendly shoulder on whom any member of his lodge can lean in times of sadness and adversity.

CHAPTER THREE

THE CHOICE OF PRAYERS

The choice of prayers for the lodge Chaplain during the usual three degrees of craft masonry are preordained by the book of ritual used by his members. The following are the prayers most usually given in lodges under the United Grand Lodge of England.

Traditional prayer for opening the Lodge in the First Degree.

Brethren, the Lodge being duly formed, before the Worshipful Master declares it open, let us invoke the assistance of the Great Architect of the Universe in all our undertakings. May our labours, begun in order, be conducted in peace and closed in harmony. So Mote it Be.

Traditional prayer used at an Initiation.

Vouchsafe Thine aid, Almighty Father and Supreme Governor of the Universe, to our present Convention, and grant that this Candidate for Freemasonry may so dedicate and devote his life to Thy service as to become a true and faithful brother amongst us. Endue him with the competency of Thy Divine Wisdom, so that, assisted by the secrets of our Masonic Art, he may the better be enabled to unfold the beauties of true Godliness to the honour and glory of Thy Holy Name.

Traditional prayer for closing the Lodge in the First Degree.

Brethren, before the Lodge is closed, let us with all reverence and humility express our gratitude to the Great Architect of the Universe for favours already received. May he continue to preserve our Order by cementing and adorning it with every moral and social virtue. S.M.I.B.

Traditional prayer for opening the Lodge in the Second Degree.

Brethren, before the lodge is opened in the Second Degree, let us supplicate the Grand Geometrician of the Universe that the rays of heaven may shed their benign influence over us to enlighten us in the paths of virtue and science. S.M.I.B.

Traditional prayer used in the Second Degree.

We supplicate the continuance of Thine aid, O merciful Lord on behalf of ourselves and him who kneels before Thee. May the work begun in Thy name be continued to Thy glory, and ever more established in us by obedience to Thy divine precepts.

Traditional prayer for closing the Lodge in the Second Degree.

Then, brethren, let us remember that wherever we are and whatever we do, He is always with us, His all-seeing eye observes us, and whilst we continue to act in conformity with the principles of the Craft, let us not fail to discharge our duties towards him with fervency and zeal. S.M.I.B.

Traditional prayer used in the ceremony of Raising.

Almighty and eternal God, Architect and Ruler of the Universe, at whose creative fiat all things were first made, we the frail creatures of Thy providence humbly implore Thee to pour down upon this Convocation the continual dew of Thy blessing. Especially we beseech Thee to impart Thy grace to this Thy servant who now seeks to partake with us in the mysterious secrets of a Master Mason. Endue him with such fortitude that in the hour of trial he fail not, but that passing, under Thy protection, through the Valley of the Shadow of Death, he may finally arise from the tomb of transgression to shine, as the stars, for ever and ever. S.M.I.B.

Traditional prayer used at an Installation.

Vouchsafe Thine aid, Almighty Father and Supreme Ruler of the Universe, to this our solemn rite, and grant that this worthy and distinguished brother who is now about to be numbered among the rulers of the Craft, may be endued with wisdom to comprehend, judgement to define, and ability to enforce obedience to Thy Holy Law. Sanctify him with Thy Grace, strengthen him with Thy mighty power, and enrich his mind with genuine and true knowledge, that he may the better be enabled to enlighten the minds of his brethren, and Consecrate this our Mansion to the honour and glory of Thy Most Holy Name. S.M.I.B. There is a particularly nice and indeed useful prayer which is included in the Consecration ceremony of a Lodge but can easily be used in a private lodge entirely on its own and it is repeated hereunder for the enthusiastic Chaplain anxious to widen his span of traditional prayers. Used at the end of the meeting before the traditional closing prayer it will add a little extra to the proceedings.

O Lord our Heavenly Father, Architect and Ruler of the Universe, who from Thy throne behold all the dwellers upon earth, direct us in all our doings with Thy most gracious favour, and further us with THY continual help, that in all our works begun, continued and ended in Thee, we may glorify Thy Holy Name. S.M.I.B.

CHAPTER FOUR

THE FESTIVE BOARD ROLE

The principle role for the Chaplain to perform at the Festive Board is of course to give a Grace before the brethren sit down for their meal. Some Chaplains' compose their own festive board Graces' and this of course adds to the diversity and individualism of the lodge concerned.

The rather traditional grace given in most lodges is as follows:

'For what we are about to receive may the Lord make us truly thankful and ever mindful of the needs of others'.

There are many prayers of localised origin which this author has been privileged to hear and in many parts of the world such local prayers take in the industries and sometimes the ethnic groupings of the brethren concerned. Some lodges, but not by any means all sing a grace at the end of the Festive Board usually the 'Laudi Spirituali'.

Whilst not in any sense acting as an adjudicator the thinking and caring Chaplain might consider it as part of his role to speak helpfully to any brother who transgresses the line between the acceptable and unacceptable when speaking at the festive board especially so when delivering what that brother believes to be a 'funny story' which is in fact simply embarrassing to a large part of the assembled brethren. It should always be remembered that although brethren will apparently laugh at a 'risque' story many are in fact deeply shocked and offended and the overall image of the lodge in which this situation occurs is diminished accordingly. The single fact that the brethren are aware that such behaviour will bring a swift and salutary rebuke from the Chaplain will assist considerably in maintaining the happiness of both the members and their guests. Such a rebuke must of course be made privately and away from the other brethren attending the meeting.

If the situation should arise whereby the lodge is fortunate enough to have a visitor who is an ordained member of the church it is a very nice gesture to invite such a guest to give the Grace at the festive board providing of course the Master is in agreement with the invitation being made.

CHAPTER FIVE

GRACES
FOR THE
FESTIVE BOARD

Probably the best known of all graces used by Freemasons is the Laudi Spirituali which is of course the grace sung after dinner is completed. From the researches made by this author it appears to have been used by Livery Companies since the mid sixteenth century. How it found its way into regular usage in masonic circles is indeed a mystery, a mystery moreover which is most unlikely ever to be solved. That this grace is used in the vast majority of lodges both at their festive boards and also at their ladies nights cannot be denied and that grace is reprinted here for the benefit of the newly appointed Chaplain.

> For these and all they mercies given,
> We bless and praise thy name O Lord!
> May we receive them with thanksgiving,
> Ever trusting in thy word.
> To thee alone be honour, glory,
> Now and henceforth for evermore. Amen.

Another well known grace used widely at the festive board in the Royal Arch has a dual function in that the first section is said prior to the meal beginning whilst the second section is given at the conclusion of the meal whilst all the members stand on each occasion.

Grace before dinner – Benedictus benedicat – Let the blessed bless.

Grace after dinner – Benedicto benedicatur – Let the blessed be blessed.

Perhaps the most common form of grace delivered at the Festive Board is that given hereunder:

> For what we are about to receive,
> May the Lord make us truly thankful,
> And ever mindful of the wants of others.

In various parts of the country the giving of Grace before meals takes on a liberal amount of local authenticity and this author has listened to many different Graces in his travels both in this country and overseas.

Many London Livery companies have their own individual Grace which is invariably used at their Court dinners and Installation night meetings but to date and after nearly forty years in the craft this author has yet to discover a lodge which has its own specially constructed Grace but that is not of course to say than none such exist. It may well be that a deeply thinking Chaplain might well compose such a Grace to be used by his lodge in perpetuity.

There is an excellent book compiled by Carolyn Martin and published by Hodder and Stoughton the ISBN No of which is 0 340 25761 X. Its title is simply 'A Book of Graces'. This book is heartily recommended to the Chaplain who wishes to broaden his repertoire.

CHAPTER SIX

THE DEMEANOUR OF THE CHAPLAIN

The Chaplain of a lodge by his years of experience and longevity will command the respect of the more junior brethren and he has an excellent opportunity in everything he undertakes to set a first class example of the manner in which a Freemason should behave under every circumstance.

Part of the role we undertake when we move to higher office after the years of holding the more junior roles on our way to the Master's chair is to educate by example both the style and type of behaviour which is expected of the membership, not only in their lodge activities but in their overall behaviour in life. The constant example set by the senior members of the lodge should always reflect to those making their way through to the chair as being the ideal demeanour and behavioural patterns expected of a member of the lodge.

In any grouping of men there will always be extroverts and introverts and it is fully understandable that both types will by their behaviour display differing attitudes towards authority and training for that is precisely what the years between being initiated and attaining the Master's chair should be.

The frivolous young man who joins the craft and feels he can behave as he would in the outside world should be gently led by example to subdue his more extrovert activities (at least whilst participating in lodge affairs) and endeavour to acknowledge his junior status within an organization which has for more than three hundred years sought to bring about a standard in life which will benefit both the member and anyone with whom he may come into contact both in his private and business life.

Such restraining of the natural impulses of the enthusiastic and exuberant newcomer and his retraining as a junior member will in most cases eventually be welcomed even if it should prove a little difficult in the initial stages. It must be emphasised that any meeting at which the lodge members are present is for the good of everyone and not an occasion for a few 'to have a party' whilst the feelings of the remaining members are not taken into consideration.

For brother Chaplain this is an area of his duties which he can with kind words and helpful and friendly advice change for the better and he should remember that as with a child all training has to be undertaken for the betterment of the individual and their eventual place in society. A good Chaplain will learn that a few well chosen and helpful words can assist very considerably in the growth of a man into a well liked and respected brother.

The demeanour of the Chaplain must be both friendly, helpful and above all he should be seen as one whose wisdom in lodge affairs as well as the world at large can benefit the younger member, moreover his presence at a meeting should add dignity to the occasion.

CHAPTER SEVEN

THE EXTRA-MURAL ROLE IN TIMES OF ADVERSITY AND SADNESS

There is a side to the role of the Lodge Chaplain which is frequently forgotten and that is when he is called upon in times of adversity and sadness. Such occasions usually arise when a brother passes to the Grand Lodge above and the Almoner as part of his duties makes contact with the wife of the deceased member.

It is always an excellent idea for the Chaplain to accompany the Almoner on such home visits both to ascertain that the circumstances in which the remaining partner are such that she is financially stable and that she has family members who will visit regularly and generally ensure that her future wellbeing is not in doubt.

An appointment is of course absolutely essential when visiting a bereaved member's wife, but a short letter from the Lodge Almoner when the death occurs expressing the condolences of the lodge whilst also saying that about three weeks after the funeral he will make contact with her to arrange to visit her to ascertain precisely what the lodge can do to assist her in the years which lie ahead. This visit should be a friendly occasion and it may well be that either or both the Almoner and the Chaplain have met the lady concerned on numerous occasions at lodge functions over the years and that any such meeting subsequent to the funeral should not be conducted in an atmosphere of black ties and long faces. Death is, strange to say, part life and we all experience it in some way or other as we grow older.

The Almoner will of course have his usual list of questions to ask which will cover the most basic elements of a person's existence. It is always useful if one can establish the telephone number of a son or daughter in the event that contact is lost for whatever reason, for the care of remaining partner's is an ongoing facet of the role which the lodge undertakes and it is delegated down to the Almoner to carry out on behalf of the lodge for the remainder of that partner's days.

Often such help can encompass a wide range of aspects for it is surprising just how many husbands take care of the financial affairs of the family whilst the wife remains blissfully unaware of the detail of investments, securities and share-holdings. Sometimes access to a suitable financial adviser is called for and this maybe one aspect of the lodge membership where such advice is available. Simple matters such as shopping, transport generally and the future living situation may arise and the subject should be one with which the Almoner and the Chaplain are conversant or at the very least can investigate and report back to the lady concerned.

This meeting when it occurs is a good opportunity to remove the masonic regalia of the deceased brother and if the circumstances are appropriate perhaps re-sell it to another brother in the lodge. This ensures that an element of the brother's interest does not cause distress or unhappiness to the widow who is left to live out her life alone.

This author is aware of a widow who is still receiving regular visits from the Almoner of her late husband's lodge albeit that it is more than thirty years since his passing. Such is Freemasonry in action and long shall it remain so.

THE IMMEDIATE PAST MASTER

CHAPTER ONE

THE MOST DIFFICULT ROLE IN THE LODGE

It is frequently said by those who have held this office that they found it more difficult than their year as Master for they had to be word perfect throughout all the ceremonies, even those delegated by the Master to other Past Masters', so the role was a greater responsibility as a result, for it meant you had to be totally 'on your toes' and ready to meet any requirement for a word throughout the whole afternoon from the opening of the lodge until the final closing.

This requirement is frequently made more difficult if one has a very competent Master for the I.P.M. can so easily be lulled into a sense of false security especially when the Master is halfway through a ceremony and appears to be supremely confident of achieving the second half with the same degree of excellence and suddenly without any warning at all he will stop and turn his head towards you which you know means he requires a word or perhaps two or three. It is then that the I.P.M. comes into his own for to aid the Master in this situation is precisely why an I.P.M. exists.

When the lodge has a Master who has had great difficulty in learning the ritual and even on the day of his installation is still a long way from showing perfection, albeit he has tried extremely hard to master the verbiage contained in the degree workings, one is perhaps expecting a busy year of prompts and help generally and is therefore concentrating on every word rather more closely than the situation described in the previous paragraph. This author can truthfully say that having been the Master of a variety of lodges over forty plus years the office of I.P.M. was to him unquestionably the most mind concentrating of any he has held in any degree in Freemasonry.

So be ready, willing and most certainly able, for the new Master will look to you as his lifeline and you must not fail him is his moment of need. Your experience through having served a year in the Master's chair has given you a degree of confidence which the new Master has yet to achieve. To perform ceremonies perfectly in the Lodge of Instruction is one thing but to experience his first full meeting in the Master's chair with everyone looking towards the East is quite different and it does take a new Master two or three meetings to settle into his new role and thereby gain confidence before he will feel he can perhaps manage without the services of the I.P.M.

This is probably when he will need you even more, for a relaxing Master can so easily stumble over something as simple as opening the lodge, a facet he has achieved with complete accuracy many, many times before and now suddenly without warning he makes a mistake, he is of course mortified and feels he has let himself and the lodge down by his error. The I.P.M. can be of the greatest possible help in this situation by giving the Master a few words of correction in a calm quiet voice and then gently follow the Master for a few lines in hushed tones until he regains his composure.

It is quite surprising how such a situation can be corrected with calm efficiency and without the rest of the assembled brethren being aware of the contribution you have made to the Master in time of need.

CHAPTER TWO

THE STATUS OF THE I.P.M.

You now occupy as a matter of right the only office in the lodge to which you can neither be appointed or elected for to be the Immediate Past Master is an office (although strangely enough you are not of course an officer), which you achieve automatically purely as a result of having spent the previous year as Master of the lodge.

In the absence of the Master you automatically assume the chair of King Solomon once again, although if the Master's absence should be by virtue of his demise then the meeting is called by the Senior Warden and is one at which you will officiate. No one can remove you from office throughout the year of your holding the role and if there should be no one to take your place then you will remain in that position until another brother has held the Master's chair for twelve months and then by right becomes the Immediate Past Master in your stead.

The Book of Constitutions Rule 104 (f) states the following:

'The Immediate Past Master, as such, is not an officer of the Lodge. He holds his position and responsibilities by virtue of his Mastership, and retains that position until a succeeding Master becomes Immediate Past Master'. He reoccupies the position if such succeeding Master should die or cease to be a member of the Lodge while holding the position of Immediate Past Master.

In Rule 104 (g) it states 'The Immediate Past Master takes precedence in the Lodge immediately in front of the Chaplain, or, if there be no Chaplain, then immediately in front of the Treasurer'.

The office of Immediate Past Master is most decidedly an onerous role to occupy as the incumbent will observe after having served his year in office. He will as a result be more enlightened for that experience. The brother who fills this office effectively, will as a result have assisted a newly installed Master to enjoy the highest office which the lodge has in its power to confer.

It is perhaps worth mentioning at this point that if both the Master and the I.P.M. for whatever reason have to be absent from a regular meeting then the senior past master present in the lodge shall take the chair, not as many presume the once removed I.P.M. For confirmation of this fact please read Rule 119 (b) of the Book of Constitutions.

CHAPTER THREE

EVER READY, WILLING AND ABLE

In the majority of offices in a Freemasons' Lodge the incumbent is totally aware of what he has to do, and moreover when and where he has to do it. There are a few offices in the lodge such as Secretary and Treasurer where there is freedom for speech at the appropriate places in the meeting. The Organist can please himself very much in his choice of music during perambulations and background music when and if pauses occur for whatever reason during a ceremony.

The Immediate Past Master however apart from his duties in opening and closing the Volume of the Sacred Law at the start and end of the lodge meeting has no such independence for he is and remains entirely at the disposal of the Master who may or may not according to his individual wish either use the expertise and ritual knowledge of the I.P.M. or reject it in favour of his own desire to complete a ceremony entirely by himself without help, guidance or any form of assistance.

How then does a brother who has spent the last year as Master of the lodge cope with a role for which he has had no training, almost certainly no previous experience, and moreover no laid down guidelines which he can with ease follow.

A brother who is about to undertake this totally new and so far unexplained role would certainly benefit from a detailed in depth discussion with the incoming Master Elect.

They should understand very clearly between themselves when a prompt is required and the manner in which both the request as well as the response should be communicated. A quiet word or words given audibly enough for the

Master to hear but quietly enough so that the whole assembled lodge is not aware that a prompt has been given are all that is required. Believe it or not this is possible and perhaps a few trial exchanges will show to both brethren the level at which their speech should be rendered.

As with every other aspect of work within the lodge help is required by most brethren at some stage or other and the fact that such assistance can be given quietly but effectively will add to the overall ambiance of the occasion. Finally do remember you are not there to show how clever you are but rather to allow the Master to be presented in the best possible light albeit that he has a friendly experienced shoulder on which to rely should the occasion demand.

CHAPTER FOUR

ASSISTING BUT ONLY WHEN ASKED

The fine line between help and interference is difficult to gauge and in order that no friction of any sort evolves between the newly installed Master and his Immediate Past Master it is a very wise action to take for them to discuss between themselves how they are going to handle the situation whereby the Master either dries up completely or requires just the odd word or two. Most, if not all, I.P.M.'s gain an ability to know when they should say something or not but to have in place a simple signal or action which will allow the Master to tell brother I.P.M. that he is in difficulties is strongly to be recommended.

Speaking patterns differ very widely, some people speak quickly to the extent that their speech is one long sentence but when that type of person dries up it is of course far more noticeable than the person who speaks slowly requiring help. The ability of the average brain to absorb the spoken word and understand its meaning and comprehend the content of what has just been uttered has been very cleverly and accurately analysed by the advertising authorities and it may interest the reader to know that if in excess of forty five words are delivered during a thirty second advertisement (actual showing time is 26 seconds on the screen) then the listener and viewer who is of course one and the same person fails to fully comprehend what is being said as well as what is being screened.

Let us now take this factual lesson into the lodge. The Master who gabbles his ritual at a rate of knots albeit that he is both accurate and misses nothing out, does in fact deliver words which are over the heads and beyond the comprehension of the brethren listening and more importantly the candidate to whom they are intended to communicate the meaning of the ceremony in which he is participating. From the foregoing it will be realised that if we can get our incoming Master to deliver at a sensible pace he will not only be listened to and understood by the brethren but he also stands far more chance of the candidate understanding what it is that he is both saying and trying to explain.

The spin off from this piece of advice is that it also gives him a greater chance to line up in his brain the next dozen or so words so that his capacity for making fewer mistakes increases in direct proportion to his ability to limit the speed at which he delivers his ritual.

Masters come in all shapes and sizes and in all levels of intellect and ability and their success or otherwise in the chair during their year in office is in large part due to their training for this important year in their masonic life. Where it is obvious that a new Master is likely to have a problem in the area of ritual delivery it is a most helpful act on the part of the I.P.M. if he privately gets together with the new Master and rehearses both the content of the ritual as well as its speed of delivery.

Believe me the brethren will enjoy a meeting far more when what is being said can be taken in and understood rather than when a Master is word perfect but delivers his ritual at the speed of a machine gun and the vast majority of his prose goes flying over the heads of the assembled brethren and moreover the candidate is left wondering just what that ceremony was all about understanding little if anything of what was intended to be communicated.

CHAPTER FIVE

RESTRAINING YOUR IMPULSES

Having just completed your own year as Master of the lodge you have experienced just what it feels like to be in charge of lodge affairs and everything that has happened to you during the past year has given you confidence in your ability to conduct the affairs of your lodge as they should indeed be conducted.

The incoming Master is at a distinct disadvantage in such circumstances for he, unlike you, has yet to achieve those credentials of authority – oh yes we know he has been installed as Master – but so far he has yet to prove his ability to discharge the office to the satisfaction of the past masters and the brethren. This means very simply that you also have to be ultra careful in the manner in which you discharge your role as the Immediate Past Master.

The new Master will of course take your word as to when he should and moreover when he should not do this or that and friendly advice is of course always welcome but it should be remembered that good helpful intentions can develop into instructions if not most carefully phrased and controlled. Remember the Master is in charge now, your year is over, and you sit at his left hand side only because you were the most recent holder of the office of Master and for no other reason. At no time do we ever want the Master to feel he is being forcibly instructed what to do even if that means you have to wait for him to ask you 'what comes next' for in this situation you are responding to a call for help which is quite different from acting as an instructor to a very new pupil.!!

Try if you can to remember just how you felt when you occupied the Master's chair for the first time and presuming you are able to do that you may perhaps realise just how insecure the new Master feels at this time. He will grow into office during his year of that you may be sure and the person who leaves the chair in twelve months time will be quite different from the brother who stepped into it so very recently. Your relationship during this crucial twelve months will benefit the new man immeasurably if handled carefully and who knows may well develop into a stronger lifelong friendship when you are both past masters.

CHAPTER SIX

TEACHING THE LESSONS OF THE FESTIVE BOARD

This chapter has nothing to do with the learning of masonic ritual word-wise, but it does have a lot to do with the effective running of the lodge overall.

How often have we attended an Installation meeting, carried out with considerable competence, with the incoming Master installing his officers to a high degree of proficiency but who, upon arriving at the Festive Board, finds himself confronted with the official toast list and looks at it as though it is written in Chinese, having not a clue as to the correct pronunciation of the names or moreover the content of the list itself or for that matter who does what and when?

He has apparently not received any instruction whatsoever on the manner in which he should propose the various toasts. Which should be grouped together, and which honorific titles should or should not be included.

How is it possible for a Master to arrive at the highest office in the lodge after possibly some ten to fifteen years of membership and be so patently ill-equipped for the task which confronts him?

We have now arrived at the point of this Chapter which is the training of the Master-Elect in general, but with special emphasis upon the Festive Board. It is an excellent plan for every Master-Elect to be taken through the Festive Board proceedings from start to finish commencing with the list of those with whom he wishes to take wine. Caution an over enthusiastic Master-Elect from extending his list beyond four or five, for the object is to include everyone but not to interrupt what should be the major opportunity for the brethren to indulge in social intercourse.

The Master of a lodge has a duty to ensure that the after proceedings are conducted with dignity and due decorum and, in particular, that once he gavels silence is immediate. The over-frequent use of the gavel is to be discouraged for such use has entirely the reverse effect to that for which the festive board is held, namely to allow the brethren to join together in conversation and mutual fellowship. Further he should be told to retain the gavel in his possession at all times and not allow anyone else to use it. He is the only one who has the authority to call the brethren to order whether it be in lodge or at the Festive Board.

Ideally the taking of wine should be dealt with between the first and main courses of a meal and if the following list is adopted we are quite sure it will meet with approval by the brethren and minimise the act of gavelling.

In time this will become known by the members as a short interlude in the Festive Board procedure and that once these 'takings of wine' are completed there will be no further interruption to the proceedings before the 'official toasts' are commenced after the coffee has been served.

1. The Master with everyone.
2. The Master with Grand Officers
3. The Master with the Initiate (if appropriate).
4. The Master with the Visiting Brethren.
5. The Master with the Past Masters & Officers of the Lodge.
6. The Master with the Master-elect (Election night only).

The order in which these toasts are taken may vary according to local custom and practice. Toast number 6 should only ever be used on election nights.

Turning now to the Official Toast list it is essential that the Master-Elect should be taken through it several times, perhaps starting whilst he occupies the office of Senior Warden. No Master should ever be allowed to arrive at his first Festive Board untried and untrained in the use of the Toast List. Ensure that military and honorific titles are omitted, except where civil titles and honorifics are sanctioned by local custom and practice, or are recommended by Grand Lodge or the Provincial or District Grand Lodge in which the lodge is situated.

The Master should be instructed that when giving masonic fire it is never speeded up to the point whereby there is competition to see who can finish first and the senior and perhaps older brethren are not only unable to participate but also become annoyed with the younger members for their apparent disrespect to the Sovereign, the Grand Master, the Craft in general and the Lodge in particular. The subject of 'masonic fire' if given in your lodge should be handled with great care and due decorum.

The Master-Elect should be reminded that it is his duty to unite and not divide the lodge. He has a heavy responsibility to ALL the members both young and old alike.

Correct teaching in the Lodge of Instruction repeatedly given throughout the year will ensure that from the most basic and indeed earliest training, the correct message is communicated at all levels.

The Master has a further duty to ensure that the Festive Board is conducted with a clear timetable in mind. The brethren have a right to expect that their time is not wasted and that the proceedings will be conducted with the minimum of time-consuming activities so that those who have trains to catch or long journeys to make are not forced to leave before the proceedings are ended.

The ideal length of speeches, when given, should be no longer than three to four minutes. Longer speeches will frequently result in brethren turning to their neighbours to talk and the courtesy and dignity of the occasion is lost.

On occasions of particular merit, the meeting may well be enhanced by the visit of a Provincial or District Grand Master, his Deputy or one of his Assistants.

When this occurs the visiting officer will usually be accompanied by a Provincial or District Grand Director of Ceremonies who will take charge of the proceedings, ceremonially speaking, and this will usually include a large part of the Festive Board.

Such Directors of Ceremonies will of course introduce the Official he has brought and it is appropriate for the Master of the Lodge to have a SHORT speech of welcome prepared for use on such an occasion, rather than to make the stark announcement that: 'We will now drink a toast to'..without any speech of welcome being given. Further, it is essential that the Master should know the correct pronunciation of the official's name and the exact rank he holds.

It assists considerably in the projection of the Lodge image for the visiting officer to see and appreciate the fact that the Master himself has taken the time and trouble to prepare his work for the Festive Board with both care and consideration for his guests, of both high and low rank alike.

Finally we trust that Brother I.P.M, will appreciate the importance of such Festive Board training and ensure that it is included in his overall plan for the year of work. It cannot be stated too clearly or too often that to have an excellent ccremony performed within the lodge room but followed by an uncontrolled and ill-prepared Festive Board is a great disappointment to both the members and their guests, and all members like to impress their guests .

Moreover it demonstrates most glaringly that the Master has put all his effort into learning the ritual, but for the remainder of his responsibilities at the lodge meeting he has received little if any training whatsoever and that training – Brother I.P.M. – is entirely 'down to you'.

CHAPTER SEVEN

AND THEY DIDN'T EVEN SAY "GOODBYE"

The Installation night on which Brother I.P.M. hands his collar of office over to the Master whom he has been supporting, guiding and generally caring for during the past year must bring forth a series of emotions amongst which will be sadness at relinquishing his role and yet joy at the thought of no longer having the responsibility for following every word of each degree worked. He may perhaps have a slight feeling of satisfaction that his progression from his first appointment probably as a Steward has now come to an end and that it has all been satisfactorily carried through, it may of course be some years before he moves into a more senior role within the lodge, so with what can he now usefully occupy his time .

Having been very much in the limelight for a goodly number of years it might perhaps suit the recently made redundant I.P.M. to give some thought to the way in which he can most effectively serve the lodge in the years which lie ahead. It might perhaps be in the area of the Lodge of Instruction or in the more personalised area of helping a brother who is experiencing particular difficulty with the ritual and really requires a one-to-one teaching and learning situation to progress in any way at all. A further thought might be to accompany out of the lodge any masonically younger brethren when a higher degree is being worked so that a rapport can be established.

One should never forget that the early days of a newly made entered apprentice will reflect his attitude to all things masonic in his later years within the lodge and such personal contact with a senior member of the lodge together with the act of spending time with him to answer the myriad of questions which all newly initiated brethren unquestionably want to ask can go a very long way to impressing the younger man or men that Freemasonry really is a caring organization which looks after its membership even from their earliest days in the lodge.

There are many roles which the Installed Master of many summers can fulfil to the overall benefit of the lodge and in so doing he ensures that the brethren to whom he is devoting time will in their turn make themselves available when they too have passed through the Master's chair and are then able to devote some of their time to assisting recently initiated and newer members as they themselves were helped in their formative years.

It will come as no surprise to the now redundant I.P.M. that no one said 'goodbye' when he finally completed his last official office. The reason for that is quite clear, he still has a large amount to contribute to the lodge and its membership in the years which lie ahead so its not 'goodbye' but rather 'hello' to a new member of the fully trained and experienced brethren which every lodge needs if it is to function to the maximum benefit of all its brethren. You are now a senior member and your hard earned experience over many summers is worth much to your lodge, make sure you use it wisely.

THE
PAST MASTERS

CHAPTER ONE

NO!
YOU ARE NOT
SUPERFLUOUS

Surprising as it may seem and probably totally unexpected by the latest recruit to the list of Past Masters a whole new world of opportunities await the experienced Past Master joining their ranks, yes we are talking about you.

The majority of years spent from taking one's first office as a Steward through to the final responsibility as Immediate Past Master have been ordered, organised and principally preordained by the ritual book and the customs prevailing in your lodge, which over the years have almost become landmarks. As far as you were concerned this meant very simply that you had a role to perform and the words to allow you to do so were already in existence. You have now entered a totally new field where your individuality can be exercised as a matter of free will on your part without any preset rules to guide you.

Your masonic experience gained through years of work both within your own lodge and visits to others will have left an invaluable amount of experience on which you can draw for the benefit of both newly initiated members as well as those who are making their way up the ladder to the Master's chair.

Let us start to evaluate the possible ways in which your ability and knowledge can be usefully assimilated by those you wish to help and those who seek your assistance in their progress through the lodge including of course those members who are already past masters but have not had the benefit of your wide ranging experience.

First and foremost a past master who is without official office can and should make himself readily available when a masonically young brother has to retire from the lodge because a higher degree is about to be worked. The three quarters of an hour spent with an inexperienced brother can be used to considerable advantage, firstly in getting to know the brother concerned during which his interests, his background and his expectations in masonry can be evaluated and generally promoted. Many young men on joining freemasonry assume quite wrongly that once they have learned the book of ritual used by the lodge they can consider themselves to be fully equipped Freemasons ready to address any situation which might present itself in their future membership of the craft. As of course is well known learning the ritual is but a beginning of their knowledge but many see it as a conclusion of their learning process. This is of course an excellent starting point on which to begin the formation of a newly initiated brother's overall learning curve.

Try to ascertain what the brother concerned feels he is achieving from his regular visits to the Lodge of Instruction and if he finds the process daunting in any way, explain that the learning of masonic ritual is a gradual process and can with many people take some years before a degree of perfection is achieved and that individual study plus regular attendance at the Lodge of Instruction will in due time make everything clear to him. Explain next that you are available for the individual answering of questions and queries should he at any time not be able to secure the necessary information from his proposer or seconder to whom he should of course first turn when such information is needed. We very frequently find that a candidate for freemasonry is proposed by an equally newly initiated brother whose own knowledge is scant and skimpy and your help will be all the more welcomed if it is made readily available as and when needed without pressure of any kind on your part to use such a facility.

The process described above will engender a worthwhile relationship with the brother concerned which will last for the rest of your conjoint masonic careers and it is very likely to be something which the new brother remembers for the rest of his masonic life for experiences such as have been described on an impressionable new member will go a long way to show in the most tangible way possible just what a friendly caring organization he has joined.

There is yet a second way in which a knowledgeable past master can be of use to the newer members of the lodge and this is by making oneself available when a junior member wishes to propose a potential candidate for membership but does not have the necessary seconder or senior member available to interview such a candidate prior to a form of application for membership being completed.

In such circumstances it is a wise move on the part of the junior member to seek help, assistance and confirmation that his choice of the potential new member and his belief that such a person will make a good member are well founded. Clearly at this stage of possible membership the proposer would like to have the wisdom and experience of a senior past master vested in the selection process for he will want confirmation that his recommendation will meet the criteria demanded of all new members to your lodge. The manner in which you deal with this situation will determine as well as educate the junior member in the art of interviewing prospective candidates and will probably stay with your junior member for the rest of his masonic life.

Turning now to a completely different aspect of assistance one can always assist the Almoner in his work and indeed if the existing Almoner is of advancing years understudy him with a view perhaps of aspiring to the office when the current incumbent feels the time has arrived to retire after many years in that demanding office. Going with the Almoner when he visits either brethren or the widows of past brethren can be a very good starting point for when one takes over such an office and an already existing portfolio of cases it is as well if one has first hand knowledge of the details of each case before being appointed.

It may well be that brother Past Master has aspirations to be of use in one of the three main areas of responsibility within the lodge namely administration, financial or ceremonial, in each case working alongside the Secretary, Treasurer or Director of Ceremonies will bring you into closer contact with all the members than has perhaps been the case previously.

A few years as Assistant Secretary before taking over the role from the current incumbent will do much to educate you in the vagaries of the role. The yearly completion of the annual return to Grand Lodge or the likewise annual preparation of the installation return can both bring their individual foibles and a word or two of explanation from the existing Secretary regarding their make–up and content can be invaluable before taking the office on a permanent basis. It is also true to say that time spent with the Treasurer can lead to the gaining of knowledge especially if one has a leaning towards figures and the compilation of accounts. A good Assistant Director of Ceremonies is an invaluable asset to any lodge and when a cohesive team is established the conjoint work of the two officers ensures a smooth overall performance of the ritual for the benefit of the candidates, brethren and visitors alike.

From the foregoing few simple examples it can quickly be seen that to regard one's year of office as I.P.M. as being the end of one's usefulness is quite wrong for you have a myriad of potential opportunities readily available if only you care to look for them.

CHAPTER TWO

TEACHING THE YOUNGER BRETHREN DURING OTHER CEREMONIES

In the previous chapter we dwelt briefly on the subject of the assistance we can give to younger brethren masonically speaking when a higher degree ceremony is being carried out. What we did not do was to explain precisely how we should disseminate masonic ritual knowledge and this we shall try to do in this chapter.

Any individual entering into membership of Feemasonry will unquestionably be confused by many aspects of his initiation and if this should be perhaps only the second or third meeting which a brother has attended this might prove be an excellent opportunity to break down the ceremony into its constituent parts and then explain in a little detail exactly what those individual segments were intended to communicate to him as the candidate.

First his entry into the lodge room blindfolded, being guided by a person whom he did not know, being dressed in a manner which was quite strange to him and having to remove all forms of metal before he was allowed entry all need explanation for they all have meaning and masonic implications.

Second explain the lodge room in its constituent parts, elucidate the reasons why the Master and Wardens sit where they do and what their individual and conjoint responsibilities are overall. Teach the points of the compass as far as the seating of the principal officers are concerned and the relationship which freemasonry uses when dealing with the north, south, east and west. Explain why the candidate was kept blindfolded when introduced to the three principal officers of the lodge before he took his Obligation and why, when he had so been Obligated and the secrets of the degree had been explained and communicated he was again taken round the lodge room to meet the other principal officers this time without being blindfolded. The significance of the ceremony then starts to take on a meaning of its own and the candidate equally begins to understand why certain things occurred in the order which they did.

Move on to explain the part of the ceremony which occurred when he had resumed his normal dress and returned to the lodge and what the ancient charge was meant to communicate.

You will most assuredly have done much to educate, interest and promote the acquisition of knowledge by the newly made brother and this in its turn will lead to even more questions when he once again has to leave the lodge room whilst a higher degree ceremony is performed. Relationships formed in this way last a lifetime and moreover you will enjoy a sense of being useful even though you are now past the Master's chair and simply just another past master!

CHAPTER THREE

HELPING
THE ALMONER

Perhaps one of the more dedicated roles in which a past master can assist is that of the lodge Almoner, for without ceremony or in front of his brethren this officer carries out his duties quietly, efficiently and with considerable care for the benefit of past members their spouses and children.

It has often been said that every member of the lodge should be an 'assistant' Almoner and moreover be ready to assist whenever such help is needed. The purpose of this chapter is to show the past master how he can be of considerable help in his masonic duties both to his lodge and to his brethren and their dependants.

Almoners are probably amongst the longest serving of the lodge officers for they accumulate knowledge over many years and invariably build a case-book on each of the people for whom they are caring. Clearly this means that the Almoner must have two types of knowledge at his disposal, first he must have a full and up-to-date record of the member and the members dependants so that he can communicate quickly and easily should the need arise and furthermore be able to complete any forms which are required from any of the masonic institutions should help be required from any of those establishments. Secondly he should have a good knowledge of the way in which each of the masonic charities operate and precisely how such help can be obtained if needed. For a Master to appoint a past master to the office of lodge Almoner who has neither experience of the role he is undertaking or indeed very little knowledge of the existing case-book of cases currently being cared for is both wrong and shows a great lack of care for the brethren of the lodge and their relations. What I can hear you ask happens when an

Almoner who has served the lodge well for many years suddenly dies without warning and their is no immediate and obvious replacement available. The answer to that question is exactly why this chapter has been written.

Most lodges have a number of past masters who can best be described as 'without portfolio' in other words with no specific office to carry out. It has been my contention now for many years that every lodge should have an assistant Almoner or if you prefer an Almoner under training who, should the need arise, be well schooled in the vagaries of the role he is about to undertake and moreover know the case histories of the current members of relatives for whom the existing or late Almoner is caring.

If such a situation as described above occurs it is essential that care can continue without a break. It is also important that the lodge itself is seen as a well organised and excellently planned and structured entity, which has given thought to how the future needs of its members and their relatives can be maintained in the event of the sudden removal for whatever reason of the duly appointed and existing lodge Almoner. If such a situation should occur in your lodge and you suddenly learn that the lodge Almoner has died, is your lodge ready and able for a new man (possibly you) to take over the responsibility for the lodge Almoner's case-book?

Knowledge in any subject is gained slowly by application and to be a successful Almoner can take many years of careful assimilation of information of all types from the help that is available from the masonic charities to the responsibilities of the Department of Social Security as well as the added financial help which can be obtained from trade unions and military sources if the brother concerned had been a serving soldier, sailor or airman. There are literally hundreds of benefit societies which have funds available to meet such demands and the manner in which they can be accessed is a minefield to the inexperienced Almoner. Never assume that the Almoners role is easy just because he doesn't have a large speaking role at lodge meetings nothing could be further from the truth.

To the past master who cares about his brethren and we hope that applies to all past masters to understudy the Almoner is an excellent role to fulfil for it usually allows plenty of time to assimilate the knowledge necessary to carry out the role effectively some years in the future but perhaps most importantly that the lodge has a ready and willing past master without portfolio who now feels wanted and necessary to his lodge and moreover the lodge itself has an emergency plan in place should the need arise. If this role should appeal to you and you have the time required to carry out the duties effectively and efficiently then why not speak with the existing Almoner and see whether your offered help would be welcomed.

It may well be that such help when offered will be eagerly accepted in which case you could start to accompany the existing Almoner on his home visits and also start to learn the processes by which effective assistance can be given.

The sudden death of a member frequently brings with it a situation for which the remaining spouse is invariably completely unprepared and who does not have anyone to whom to turn for help, assistance and generally has no idea of 'what to do next'. A good lodge Almoner can in such circumstances be a stalwart friend to whom the remaining partner in a marriage can turn for guidance, help, consolation and organisation. We never know when such situations will arise and to be prepared for them when they do means we have thought ahead because we care for our brethren and their relatives and that surely is one of the all embracing tenets of our order.

CHAPTER FOUR

UNDERSTUDYING THE SECRETARY, TREASURER OR D.C.

The three principal offices of administration, finance and ceremonial are of course undertaken by the Secretary, Treasurer and Director of Ceremonies. Each of these offices has their own speciality requiring knowledge, experience and application. Of the three generally speaking only the D.C., has an assistant appointed annually by the master and occasionally one finds an assistant secretary appointed also. Brother Treasurer has no such help officially but there is no reason why all three offices cannot be understudied by a past master who remains without a portfolio to fill.

The work of Brother Secretary is diversified and complex and most secretaries of some years standing attend to their duties on a meeting by meeting basis and where necessary fill in the installation returns and annual returns without any problem whatsoever. The same can be said of the production of the lodge summons and the completion and despatch of forms for initiation and raising together with the request where applicable for a Grand Lodge Certificate. But how does a newly untrained past master cope with such duties when he finds himself plunged into office without any previous training whatsoever? Clearly this is not an ideal place to start to acquire knowledge, and the well run and forward thinking lodge will have addressed the possibility of such a situation occurring well in advance of the event happening. To train a replacement for each of the three principal offices in the lodge is highly advisable and equally shows good forward planning, moreover it allows for changes to take place without any major upheaval occurring so that the harmony and quiet efficiency of the lodge in all departments can be maintained without let or hindrance.

The lodge which runs smoothly and without major crises is hardly, if ever, noticed or appreciated by the membership and indeed this is as it should be. One cannot emphasise enough that change in any area of life is constant and it is the well planned and thought out entity which accomplishes such change without any form of disturbance to its regular routine. Well trained substitutes readily to hand are worth their weight in gold.

CHAPTER FIVE

HELPING AT THE LODGE OF INSTRUCTION

Not every lodge has a Lodge of Instruction but those which do find that the heart of the lodge resides in its regular weekly or monthly meetings which can be likened to the dress rehearsals for a major event. The actual lodge meetings themselves are of course the outward sign of the months and indeed years of private as well as communally collective training. There is of course another side to the Lodge of Instruction which is frequently not appreciated even by those attending regularly and put very simply it is the opportunity on a very regular basis for the younger as well as the established brethren to get to know each other.

If one thinks seriously about the lodge meeting itself and the amount of time that there is for general social intercourse it will be quickly appreciated that apart from those with whom one sits close to at the festive board the opportunities are of very short duration indeed hence the greater chance presented by the somewhat less authoritarian atmosphere of the Lodge of Instruction. To meet with ones brethren in a happy, relaxed environment allows for greater personal interplay between individuals and as a result stronger bonds are formed which invariably last for many many years.

How then can a past master help at such a regular event as the weekly or monthly Lodge of Instruction? First there is the obvious role to fill as the preceptor or assistant preceptor both roles require dedication and patience of goodly proportions. Brethren should always be guided in the perfection of the office to which they are aspiring, never 'drilled' the kindly words of help plus where necessary being shown first hand how some move or other should be achieved goes a long way to making a somewhat unsure new member feel more confident about his ability to cope with the demands made upon him within the lodge both currently and perhaps more importantly in the years which lie ahead. It is very easy for an experienced past master to forget his somewhat nervous first attempts at carrying out an office in the L.O.I., perhaps made twenty, thirty or even forty years ago. Not only is this type of help invaluable it also helps newer members to establish themselves in their somewhat strange new environment.

Every Lodge of Instruction requires a secretary to record the evenings work and in this department your attendance can release a lay brother to take office where he might have been seconded to the secretary's desk. The presence of past masters' at the Lodge of Instruction shows to the newer members in a way which cannot be bettered just how much membership of the order means to those who have been through the master's chair and yet still attend the Lodge of Instruction to help those who are making their way through the offices of the lodge.

Yes, your regular attendance can be of the greatest possible help particularly when there are vacancies to fill especially if the preceptor or his assistant is not able to be present on any particular evening. Some Lodges of Instruction appoint two preceptors so that the burden of regular weekly attendance can be lessened and that the brethren do not suffer for want of training or guidance.

The Lodge of Instruction is where the lodge grows candidates into members and this should never be forgotten for properly run it can be one of the lodge's most valuable assets.

CHAPTER SIX

THE TYLER

This author is aware of a number of lodges who use their past masters in a most helpful way after they have finished their year as the Immediate Past Master of the lodge and this is by the master appointing, yes appointing such a brother to spend a year outside the door of the lodge as the lodge Tyler.

In some of the lodges where this happens it has become the custom for the brother so appointed to receive from the master a cheerful farewell ending with the words 'we all look forward to seeing you again next year'. Amusing, well of course it is but there are two other important aspects which should be remembered. First the brother so appointed will save the lodge a considerable amount of money (particularly in London) at each of the meetings and secondly it is a first hand example of teaching younger brethren that no matter how senior or important they may believe themselves to be, serving their lodge is of greater importance still and those who are willing to undertake such duties are valued most highly.

It is not at all unusual in such lodges to see the stewards assisting the past master so appointed both prior to and at the closure of the lodge in the laying out and subsequent collection of lodge collars, gavels and other appurtenances. The maxim to be remembered of course is that many hands make light work. A rather nice and much appreciated conclusion to the brother's year as Tyler is for him to be presented with some small memento of his important year serving the lodge in the humblest of offices possible.

Service to one's lodge should be the hallmark of every member and never left to 'someone else'.

CHAPTER SEVEN

INDIVIDUAL INSTRUCTION

One area in which the past master with a little time to spare can be of the most assistance is in helping with the instruction of the brother who finds learning masonic ritual totally beyond his ability, or so he thinks.

Every individual has their own learning curve or to put it rather more simply each learns at a different speed to his neighbour and the ability to absorb verbiage does present some brethren with a magnitude of impossibility seemingly so great that they almost resign themselves to the fact that they will never, indeed cannot ever, learn the ritual no matter how hard they try.

The past master who can take on such a challenge need not be a professional teacher in any sense of the word simply a brother who is prepared to put in the time and energy to teaching very slowly an aspiring student who firstly needs his confidence boosting and then by achieving desired goals can go forward to making a useful and valuable member of the lodge. How then do we achieve this utopian dream.

When faced with a ritual book containing the three degrees of craft masonry the less than confident brother can well make the emotive, and sometimes final decision, that his knowledge of his own ability tells him he will 'never' be able to assimilate all this verbiage and that he would be far better advised to admit this now and not waste the time of others who are clearly more competent than he is. These words actually came from a man who held a Doctorate of Philosophy and who, ten years later, was an exemplary Master of his lodge.

Faced with a page of anything of some ten or twelve lines and being asked whether he could manage to learn this in a month, virtually every brother would say either 'yes' or that he would certainly do his best. Indeed few, if any would turn down that request without some consideration.

This simple but none-the-less easily demonstrated example goes a long way to showing the individual past master how to begin the task of building confidence and encouraging the aptitude of the brother who has but recently joined the Lodge of Instruction. If we examine virtually any ritual book we will find that a page does not usually exceed thirty or so lines and there is on most pages at least one break in the printed wording.

Giving a member a small paragraph to learn will usually start to build his confidence and before you move him on to the next paragraph you will find that he has of his own volition already started to read through if not indeed begun to learn that which follows.

Tell him to learn the first degree and he will almost certainly give one of the following answers: 'I do not have the time at the moment'; 'I do not have the ability to study so much ritual as I never was a good learner at school'; 'I never realized I would have to do all this when I joined the craft'; 'I will leave it until I have more time'; 'Perhaps when I have retired I will be able to consider it again'.

There are many variations to this theme but the truth is simple, you have asked for too much at one 'bite'. A couple of sentences, yes certainly one paragraph, perhaps even a short page, but twenty pages of ritual most certainly not, because it is a daunting task to almost anyone and no one, particularly a new member, wishes to look foolish in front of his friends.

What have we learned from this chapter so far? Firstly, a little at a time. Secondly, that a brother with a first class education has the same natural reticence and doubt as his less educated brother. Thirdly, success builds success which builds more success. It is important that every brother has a small task to achieve by the time of the next Lodge of Instruction meeting, no matter how small that task may seem – even learning the correct pronunciation of words can be a beneficial task to set and is most essential.

Incidentally you will get a great deal of satisfaction as well from your individual teaching of a brother who came to you as knowing nothing and moreover convinced he never would especially so when he stands up in the lodge of instruction and performs a small piece of ritual really well. The moral here is that even though you are a past master there is still a great deal of satisfaction to be gained from helping others.

CHAPTER EIGHT

PLAYING THE
WAITING GAME

The following scenario will sometimes occur and perhaps a true story of one way to handle such a situation to advantage will assist a willing past master should he ever find himself in a similar situation.

A young man in his early twenties is admitted a member of the lodge and after completing his three degrees is encouraged to attend the L.O.I. he does so and quickly finds that there is considerably more to learn than perhaps he has ever thought would be the case, if indeed he has ever thought about it at all. We should say right away that any candidate for our order should be properly briefed about his forthcoming responsibilities but in truth can one really explain to a potential new member just what the learning process will consist of without perhaps scaring away what might well be a useful addition to the lodge and to freemasonry and more importantly someone who would benefit from becoming a member of the craft.

Such a situation occurred during the writers ten-year period of Preceptorship (when he was also Secretary of his mother lodge).

A bright young man in his early twenties who was a police officer told the writer he felt that perhaps he had made a mistake in joining the lodge. He simply did not have the time to attend the Lodge of Instruction each week and as he had many years of study before him in his career he did not feel he could be the sort of member of the lodge which his proposer and seconder would wish and therefore he should, out of consideration for the lodge, resign forthwith.

This Secretary wrote to him at some length, telling him that his prime duty was to attend to his private studies and so render the future secure for himself and his family and that he should complete this process before he attempted to progress in the lodge. He stated further that no one would think any the less of him whilst he studied, sat and hopefully passed his examinations in his chosen profession.

The advice was accepted and the young man took and quickly passed his Sergeants examination and with two short years thereafter was made an Inspector. Subsequently he was seconded to the police training college at Bramshill from where he emerged some three years later as a Chief Inspector. He later progressed to Superintendent then Chief Superintendent and now holds the rank of Commander whilst still in his mid-forties.

Once through his Inspectors' examination and with his hardest study behind him, but with a brain which had been dedicated to study and learning for a number of years, he started to read and practice the ritual used by his lodge. As a result he became one of the finest Masters the lodge had experienced for many years. He has now completed a two-year period in charge of his mother Chapter and thoroughly enjoyed the experience, performing the ceremony with considerable ability and assurance. We now have an experienced lodge and chapter officer still under fifty with many years to serve in any office to which he is appointed.

This is a true story told without any exaggeration whatsoever. The moral here is very clear. Push a young man too hard whilst he has his mind set on making his way in the world and you could well lose a first class master of ten years hence.

Be far sighted with your planning and care for the whole member not just his masonic attendance and you will not only produce a good lodge officer and eventually a first class Master but you will have also made a firm friend for life.

The other and perhaps most important message you will also have communicated is that Freemasonry cares about its members, their families and their future.

A past master who takes the time and trouble to get to know his members well by understanding those things which motivate them and those mountains they have to climb, metaphorically speaking, will be dealing with the whole man and not just that part of him which appears on masonic occasions.

Remember that we all have many facets to our lives involving many different emotions which can and do motivate us. Without wishing to turn every past master into a clinical psychologist the more we can stand back a little and look at what is best for the 'whole' man rather than that part we wish to see serve our needs in the lodge the happier will be our lodge as well as the member about whom we have thought deeply.

Freemasonry cares about its members, their families and their dependants and it hurts not at all to let the whole world be aware of this basic and fundamental facet of our order.

CHAPTER NINE

MAKING
FRIENDS FOR LIFE

It is doubtful if there is one freemason in the craft today who cannot remember with crystal clarity the Preceptor or Preceptors of his Lodge of Instruction, together with the nuances which they used, their gentle or harsh methods of explanation and training and their friendly word of help when things clearly were not going as well as the brother under training had hoped.

It is perhaps unnecessary and even trite to remind the reader that Freemasons come from every type of background. Educational ability and strength in one sphere is in no way an automatic guarantee for success in ritual ability or performance. Such perfection, if indeed perfection it is, comes from dedication in reading, regular rehearsal and generally absorbing what is after all a totally new style or type of language for the vast majority of those embarking on their masonic careers. It really is quite surprising how often from a level start those enthusiastic brethren who truly dedicate themselves can and will make giant strides in progress and ritual retention.

One such example is told principally because it is quite true but more so because it had side effects which no one including this Preceptor ever thought possible. A candidate for initiation came before the Committee of Management for interview regarding his admission into the lodge. During the interview he demonstrated that he had a stutter of considerable proportions, which clearly embarrassed him. This stutter became much worse when responding to questions put by the dozen or so members of the committee. Naturally this difficulty was mentioned during the ensuing discussion relative to his ever being able to hold office. The candidate met the basic rules for admission into our order and was subsequently initiated and thereby became a member of the lodge.

Subsequent discussion ensued after he had been raised and his entry to the L.O.I, became imminent. What if anything could this brother achieve? Would he and perhaps the brethren be embarrassed by his pronounced stutter which on occasions reduced him almost to a 'non-speaking jelly'?

The Preceptor invited this newly raised brother to join him the following week and placed him in a seat next to himself, explaining the various sections of the ceremony under rehearsal. This continued for many weeks without the new entrant making any attempt or indeed being invited to fill an office, albeit he tried to give the VSL closing ritual and had great difficulty.

This Preceptor gradually got to know the new brother on a one to one basis and after a number of weeks was invited by his new recruit to 'come home for coffee' one evening after the L.O.I. finished.

Almost immediately he was inside his own front door the stutter all but disappeared and within the portals of his own home he was, speech-wise, a very different man from the one who had been struggling with just a small passage at the L.O.I. an hour earlier.

We tried a private experiment without telling the rest of the members of the L.O.I. This was a simple but effective part answer to his problem. We asked the brother to take a view of his living room in his mind and when he had a portion of ritual to deliver to close his eyes, bring the vision of his living room into his mind and deliver the ritual. Within two or three weeks everyone but everyone was making comments on his progress, such comments as 'his stutter has all but disappeared'.

Could he ever make a competent lodge officer? Subjective views were aired and eventually with some obvious relief by all concerned it was decided to 'leave the situation in the hands of the Preceptor' to advise the Master of the year whether or not he thought Bro — would be able to carry out the offices without causing embarrassment to himself or disrupting the dignity which we try to maintain in all the ceremonies we carry out.

Without wishing to prolong this story let us come to the end result, which was surprising to everyone of his fellow brethren.

The brother concerned quickly made progress simply because he had proved to himself that he was capable of learning the ritual. What was more he recited it back with considerable ability and with only the very occasional slight stutter which could generally be related to the small amount of stress which he was undergoing at that moment. Thus it had been determined quite clearly that his stutter was stress-related.

His overall ability to speak without stuttering amongst his family and friends improved immeasurably. He went on to become a useful member of his local community by serving as a councillor and eventually becoming the Chairman of a sub-committee which meant many speeches and control of meetings, something he would never have dreamed of when he joined the lodge.

The moral here is obvious. The brother of whom we write had gained confidence in his own ability by the simple lesson of getting him to feel relaxed and comfortable. The answer to his problem had been within his own home all the time, for there he felt secure, totally relaxed and comfortable and when he experienced all those emotions he did not stutter.

It is amazing is it not, how often the answers to our problems are sometimes staring us in the face but we do not see them until another person points them out? This author likes to feel that this brother's relationship with his brethren in Freemasonry gave him a better involvement in life generally than perhaps might otherwise have been the case. The spin-off is that this brother although now many years past the chair has never forgotten the help and advice he was given in his earliest days in Freemasonry by 'his' lodge and 'his' Preceptor of whom he has made a friend for life.

Oh! and by the way the Preceptor learned something too !

CHAPTER TEN

ADDRESSES TO THE MASTER WARDENS AND BRETHREN

It is of course the right of the Master to determine who shall participate in the ceremony of Installation of his successor and it is usually the case in most lodges that the address to the Master is given by the brother who has installed him. This however is not always the case and it is an excellent idea if the past master 'without portfolio' ensures his continuing accuracy with the ritual as his years after the masters chair start to accumulate for to have a ready and willing past master available to participate by giving one of the three addresses is of great assistance to any Master wanting to ensure that his 'hand over' meeting ends a first class year in charge of the lodge affairs.

The various rituals used in English and Welsh craft masonry carry the same basic sentiment so although the words may be a little different the message and meaning remain the same.

For a Master about to install his successor it is a great comfort to have a friendly willing and capable past master available to carry out each of the addresses which he the Master does not wish to undertake on the night he installs his successor. In many lodges it is the custom for the Master to deliver the address to the incoming master and in the following year to give the address to the wardens and in the third year to complete his triumvirate of addresses by giving that to the brethren. A Master who can accomplish the three addresses successfully can indeed consider his period in office to have been very satisfactory andfurthermore incoming future masters will remember with pleasure the man who is ready willing and capable to be called upon when needed who can be relied upon to render the task requested in a first class manner.

The final point in this chapter is that for a past master to be asked to perform any task of this nature especially when his year in the chair is long past shows that he is wanted, needed and most of all not forgotten.

CHAPTER ELEVEN

ORGANISING THE LADIES NIGHT

Ladies Nights have existed for many years and their format varies in different parts of the country. It is also true to say that their size and content has varied over the years since the end of World War Two. Cost is of course a major consideration these days and some lodges particularly in London find that a weekend at the south coast which encompasses Friday night until Sunday lunchtime staged in a good hotel has more support than the simple annual evening out which prevailed for many years after world war two.

There is of course another quite simple explanation of the popularity of such events these days and that is directly linked with the ability of the car driver to enjoy a little alcoholic refreshment whilst not having the need to go anywhere near his car for driving purposes.

The past master who has a natural inclination towards organization will thrive on the prospect of being in charge of arranging the lodge Ladies Night for it once again allows him to feel needed, wanted and moreover not regarded as yesterday's man. Arrangements for such an occasion do of course have to start very early in the annual masonic calendar for the booking of a suitable hotel and the arranging of costs and meal details all of which require good management skills if they are to be concluded in such a manner as to allow a reasonable ticket price.

A wise past master will if asked by the Master form a small sub committee of possibly three brethren each of whom should have designated tasks to fulfil, such as the printing of tickets and table place names, the hire of the band and any entertainers required and negotiations with the hotel concerned on the timing and content of the meal to be provided. Some lodges indulge in raffles on such occasions but this is an area which should be carefully organized if it is not to upset those attending.

Ladies Nights are by tradition happy occasions and this should be the constant thought behind anything which is arranged for the Ladies benefit. We would always want them to depart from such an occasion remembering a hapy well organized event which they will look forward to when the following year the occasion is repeated.

A past master who has both the organizational skills and ability to carry through such an event is a valuable asset to any lodge and we would heartily recommend any past master 'without portfolio' to consider how he might be able to help in this one evening in the annual life of the lodge.

CHAPTER TWELVE

TEACHING THE STEWARDS HOW TO PERFORM THEIR ROLE CORRECTLY

It really is surprising just how often we see a newly appointed steward being allowed to undertake his duties without any instruction whatsoever, he appears to have no idea of what he is supposed to do albeit that he has attended many meetings before and been served by stewards on each occasion.

It is always a sensible idea to allow a past master to undertake the overall supervision of the stewards especially where they are inexperienced or totally lacking in the knowledge to allow them to carry out their tasks correctly.

Let us start with the pouring of wine, this should always be accomplished by the steward first asking the intended recipient of his choice of liquid refreshment and he should most certainly not interrupt any conversation which the person to whom he is catering may be having with his neighbour. When a choice has been established the wine should be poured leaving at least an inch from the top of the wine to the top of the glass. When the pouring is completed and before the steward takes the bottle or decanter away it should be twisted to ensure that no drip ensues from the lip of the aforesaid receptacle. Let us move on to the next stage of wine pouring which is when the steward is required to refill the glasses of those who have partaken. Always ask if the person whose glass is about to be refilled if they require a further quantity of wine for very often one can witness an untrained steward automatically refill the glass of a member or guest without any authority or wish on the part of that person to have his glass refilled. It is the duty of every member to ensure that those who are driving are capable of doing so and that the over imbibing of alcohol does not turn what was intended to be a happy evening into one whereby the guest of a member ends up having a conversation with an officer of the law.

Moving on to another task which is frequently left to the lodge stewards to perform and here I refer to the selling of raffle tickets. Any member or guest has an equal right to say yes to a purchase or no as the case may be and it is not the duty of the steward to press anyone, member or guest alike, to purchase something which they do not wish to have.

Sadly this author whilst an Assistant Provincial Grand Master with some fifty lodges under his care witnessed elderly brethren, many of whom may well have been living on a retirement pension and little else, being pressed into buying raffle tickets which they could patently not afford with money which might well have been intended for some other important purpose. Therefore if it should be that you are charged with training the stewards of your lodge remind them that Freemasons come in all sizes and all financial levels and the few pounds which the steward might consider small might well be an elderly member's lunch the following day. Stewards should care for visitors to the lodge whose host has not yet arrived, there can scarcely be a worse starting point to a visit than for the guest to be left staring at the wallpaper because his host has been delayed by either road traffic or trains from arriving at the appointed time for their meeting.

Remember and remember well that first impressions remain with visitors, and the friendly warm welcome made by a Steward upon the arrival of a guest to the lodge will do much to enhance the image and vision of your lodge in the eyes of the invited guest and moreover the host will thank them as well.

CHAPTER THIRTEEN

THE GRAND LODGE CERTIFICATE

The presentation of a Grand Lodge Certificate to the new member upon his having taken his third degree is an important milestone in that new member's masonic career for it will only happen to him once during his life in Freemasonry, for although he may well seek and be accepted for other orders in Freemasonry he will only ever get one Grand Lodge Certificate. The brother therefore who delivers it into the safe keeping of the new member undertakes a most vital and extremely important role for the Master and one which should not be undertaken unless the past master concerned is fully competent to do so.

Many but not all rituals have their own version of the presentation of a Grand Lodge Certificate but there is no 'official' delivery version produced by Grand Lodge. All delivery versions follow a similar format giving a brief explanation of the signs, symbols and meaning of the content of the Certificate much of which the person to whom the Certificate is being given will not remember and it is for that reason that this author adopted a simple but effective means of ensuring that the candidate to whom the certificate was being presented did not leave the lodge room that evening without being handed a small booklet in which there was a full explanation of the Certificate and its history. Over many years this author presented many many Certificates and on every occasion the candidate was asked to promise to read the booklet when he was at home with his Grand Lodge Certificate open in front of him so that he could visibly appreciate exactly what was written in the booklet. It was interesting to note that brethren have come up to this author ten fifteen and some more years than that after being so presented with their Certificate and have mentioned how useful this small booklet was in learning something of 'their' very special Grand Lodge Certificate. The booklets are available from most masonic suppliers and are within the orbit price wise of every Freemason. I commend this practice to anyone who is charged with the delivery of the Grand Lodge Certificate to a new member.

Always remember to mention to the brother who is being so presented that he is now qualified to join the Holy Royal Arch which will provide the culmination of his qualifications.

CHAPTER FOURTEEN

A 'TOUCH ON THE TILLER'

Finally we reach the end of the section on the duties which a past master can carry out albeit he has not been given an official office in the lodge. In addition to the many ways in which a past master can contribute to the lodge he can also deliver the explanation of the working tools when requested to do so, it relieves the Master of a small part of the ceremony and the change of voice very frequently is appreciated.

Most past masters having finished their year as Immediate Past Master feel they are no longer wanted, required and are superfluous to requirements, it is hoped that through the perusing of the previous fourteen chapters the reader will now realise that there are many many ways in which he can be of use to his lodge, his current Master and also to the up and coming brethren who in years to come will, like him, be past masters as well. Learning any lesson in life by example is probably the finest manner in which it can be learnt and the past master who shows also by example that his days at the top of the lodge tree have not left him feeling unwanted and unnecessary for there are a myriad of other tasks which can be undertaken if the mind is applied. Moreover it will help to keep the slightly older and perhaps retired past master active together with a feeling of being wanted and necessary. It is those members of our order who keep their brains as well as their bodies active who enjoy life to the greatest extent and remember there are always others surrounding you in your community who would benefit from an hour or so in conversation for loneliness in old age in surely the greatest burden of all.